BUREAU OF LAND MANAGEMENT

California
Desert
District

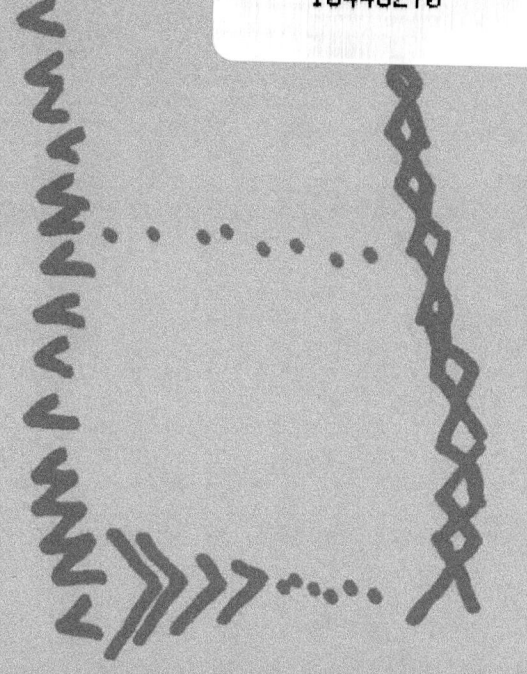

The Cahuilla and the Santa Rosa Mountain Region: Places and their Native American Association

by
Lowell John Bean,
Sylvia Brakke Vane,
and Jackson Young

RUSSELL L KALDENBERG - SERIES EDITOR

cultural resource publications

anthropology - history

Cover illustration of pictograph in the Santa Rosa Mountains from a slide taken by Robert Laidlaw. Illustration by Jim Carrol.

FOREWARDS

This ethnographic overview represents a significant and innovative contribution to studies of culture history in the California Desert. The authors have succeeded in synthesizing archival and contemporary materials into a unique ethnographic research document. A number of systems models have explored the interaction between the Native Populations of the Southern California and the physical environment in which their cultures developed. This volume contributes significantly to understanding these human relationships to the land and its resources in a portion of traditional Cahuilla territory. We offer special thanks to the Native American consultants who in conjunction with the efforts of Dr. Lowell Bean, Sylvia Brakke Vane and Jackson Young, made this report possible.

Robert M. Laidlaw
Anthropologist
Bureau of Land Management,
Sacramento, CA

I wish to thank all of those who have supported the archaeology program in the California Desert in its efforts to print and disseminate cultural resource data to the general and professional public. Among those are, Gerald Hillier, Bruce Ottenfeld, Bary Freet, Ronald Keller, and Bill Olsen. A special note of thanks goes to Clara Stapp who did the petroglyph drawing from a photograph taken by Robert Laidlaw. I hope that in these days of constrained budgets that the reprinting and dissemination of Cultural Resource Reports will be further accomplished and encouraged by management and staff alike.

Russell L. Kaldenberg
Cultural Resource Program Manager
Cultural Resources Publications
Series Editor
California Desert District

THE CAHUILLA AND THE SANTA ROSA MOUNTAIN REGION:

PLACES AND THEIR NATIVE AMERICAN ASSOCIATIONS

A Review of Published and Unpublished Sources

Prepared

by

CULTURAL SYSTEMS RESEARCH, INCORPORATED

for

UNITED STATES DEPARTMENT OF INTERIOR
BUREAU OF LAND MANAGEMENT
CALIFORNIA DESERT PLANNING PROGRAM
3610 Central Avenue, Suite 402
Riverside, California 92506
Contract No. CA-960-C-79-104

Contributing Scholars:

Lowell John Bean, Ph.D.

Sylvia Brakke Vane, M.A.

Jackson Young, B.A.

Submitting Officers and
    Editors:

Lowell John Bean, Ph.D.
President, CSRI

Sylvia Brakke Vane, M.A.
Vice President, CSRI

RUSSELL L. KALDENBERG
SERIES EDITOR

FIRST PRINTING
RIVERSIDE, CALIFORNIA
OCTOBER 1981
300 Copies

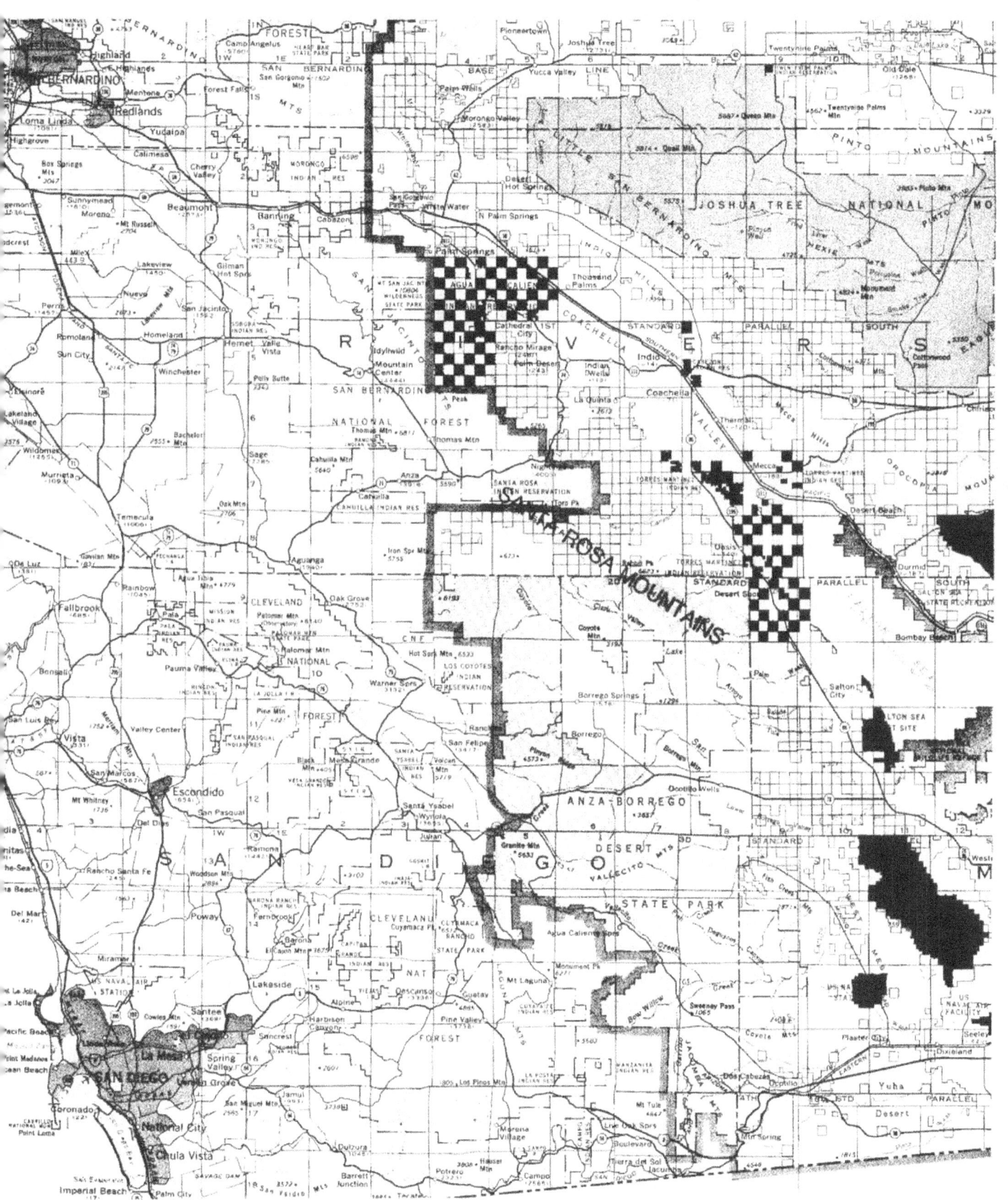

Bureau of Land Management base map indicating the relationship of the study area to Southern California.

CHAPTER I. INTRODUCTION

This report on places of archaeological, ethnographic, and ethnohistoric interest within a portion of traditional territory of the Cahuilla Indians has been prepared by Cultural Systems Research, Incorporated, for the U.S. Department of the Interior, Bureau of Land Management (BLM), Desert Planning Staff, Riverside, California, under Purchase Order CA-960-C-79-104, issued November 8, 1978. The research was directed and the report was by Lowell John Bean, Ph.D., and Sylvia Brakke Vane, M.A. Mr. Jackson Young, field ethnographer, assisted in archival research and mapping. Native Americans who participated in this study included Mrs. Katherine Siva Saubel of Los Coyotes Indian Reservation, Mrs. Alice Lopez and Mr. Vergil Lawson of Torres-Martinez Indian Reservation, and Mr. Anthony Andreas of Agua Caliente Indian Reservation.

Katherine Siva Saubel is a member of the Los Coyotes Indian Reservation. She resides at Morongo Indian Reservation. She is a member of the Isilsiva lineage. She is approximately 58 years of age, fluent in the Cahuilla language, and extremely knowledgeable about the ethnography and history of the Cahuilla people.

Alice Lopez is a member of the Torres-Martinez Indian Reservation in Imperial County. She is the step-daughter of Francisco Toro, and was wife of the late Cahuilla shaman Salvador Lopez. She is approximately 80 years of age, fluent in Cahuilla and extremely knowledgeable about the culture and history of the Cahuilla people.

Anthony Andreas is of the Paniktum lineage and a member of the Agua Caliente Indian Reservation. He is active in contemporary Cahuilla affairs and expert in the Cahuilla culture and history of his area.

Mr. Vergil Lawson is a member of the Torres-Martinez Indian Reservation and a descendant of the Cahuillas of the Colorado Desert.

CSRI received special assistance from Dr. Eric Ritter and ethnographer Robert Laidlaw of the BLM Desert Planning Staff who provided generously of their time and assistance for this project.

The purpose of this research has been to put together data on the cultural resources of the Santa Rosa Mountains and associated parts of the California desert as part of a larger study presently being conducted by the Bureau of Land Management Desert Planning Staff. This larger study is directed toward the identification and evaluation of Native American traditional use areas, ritually associated resource localities, and sacred locations or areas, so that these Native American sites under the jurisdiction of the Bureau of Land Management can be identified, evaluated, and protected. The research results will also assist the Bureau of Land Management to make sure that projects initiated by the Bureau or actions coming under its jurisdiction do not inadvertently harm or destroy cultural resources.

These data then are designed to be used in a desert-wide land use allocation plan for the California Desert Conservation Area, an area likely to be seriously threatened by the rapidly growing population of southern California. The Study Area includes selective locations in the Santa Rosa Planning Units of Riverside County and small portions of San Diego and San Bernardino Counties (see attached maps). Emphasis is placed on vacant public domain within the California desert in and adjoining the Santa Rosa Mountains.

In addition to meeting the above listed objectives, this study provides a considerable amount of new information regarding Cahuilla land use and occupancy. The study provides new interpretations of data available from various sources, which are here for the first time placed in a single context. The material will be useful to scholars who wish to study Cahuilla land use and occupancy in greater depth.

CSRI has examined the published and unpublished ethno-graphic literature on the Native Americans known to have been associated with the Study Area. These are principally the Cahuilla Indians, but the Serranos have been associated with the western secondary Study Area, and in the historic period the Chemehuevis have been associated with the Study Area in that they live in the towns and reservations in Coachella Valley near the Primary Study Area. We have noted and mapped the sites recorded in the literature as being named, used, or told about in oral literature by Native Americans. Each site was given a number as it was encountered in the literature.

Duplicate sites and most of those outside the Study Area were later deleted from the list.

In Chapter II of this report, the principal areas of occupation and use are discussed in some depth, beginning with the western Secondary Study Area and proceeding to sites to the south and west. In Chapter III, descriptions of sites, in alphabetic order, and comments on their significance are given, with reference when appropriate to discussions in Chapter II. A table of sites in numerical order is also included. This table also indicates what recorded archaeological sites are associated with a site or area that has been discussed.

Our theoretical position is drawn from cultural ecology and general systems theory. Stress is put on the importance of the natural environment to the Native American, with respect both to its effect on traditional social and cultural patterns, and to its present-day role in the maintenance of ethnic identity patterns. Our theoretical position is given in considerable detail in two recent publications (Bean and Vane 1978:2-1 to 2-13; 1979:2-1 to 2-7).

The Study Area consists for the most part of the mountainous areas ringing the Coachella Valley. Some information about valley sites outside the Study Area has been included when necessary to explain the ethnographic data.

10-12-77   30,000   BLM CALD-77   1-8 №

Overflight photograph taken at 30,000 feet of Martinez Canyon as it meets
Coachella Valley. Scale approximately 1"=2 miles. Original on file at the
California Desert District Office of the Bureau of Land Management, Riverside,
California.

CHAPTER II. THE ETHNOGRAPHY OF THE STUDY AREA: A NARRATIVE

A Brief History of the People in the Area

The study area (as outlined on Map 1) was occupied in the time of European contact by various political units of the Takic-speaking peoples, mainly the Cahuilla. They were at that time divided into approximately a dozen indenpendent corporate politico-religious kin groups (clans). These clans owned large tracts of territory, each of which included several ecological zones. The tracts usually included areas at both higher and lower elevations so that people could take advantage of the wide variety and seasonality of floral and faunal resources (Bean 1972).

Clans were further divided into lineages which were also corporate groups. Each clan was composed of from two or three to a dozen lineages. Each lineage occupied a particular village site, and also owned specific tracts of land within the clan territory for hunting, gathering, and other purposes. In historic times two or more lineages sometimes occupied one village site. Very often a lineage occupied a specific canyon. Thus the paniktum lineage occupied portions of Andreas Canyon. On the other hand, Santa Rosa Canyon was occupied by an entire clan in the late nineteenth century.

Cahuilla clans were organized around a hierarchical religious and political structure. Each clan had one or more ceremonial units (an official, a ceremonial house, and a

ceremonial bundle). The ceremonial unit served as the symbolic representation of the sociopolitical reality of the
group. These units were part of a larger integrative system
(ritual congregation) which connected many politically auto-
nomous groups into a wider religious, economic, and political
network of cooperative groups (Bean 1972).

The Cahuilla lived for the most part by hunting and
gathering, although there is some indication that agricultural techniques were used prior to European contact. The
hunting and gathering techniques were sufficiently developed
that some authors have suggested that they enjoyed a quasi-
agricultural subsistence technology (Lawton and Bean 1968).

The Cahuilla had well established political marriage and
trade relationships with all of their neighbors, being allied
with the Gabrielino toward the coast and the Halchidoma on
the Colorado River. They intermarried with and traded frequently with the Diegueño, the Luiseño, the Serrano, the
Chemehuevi, and even the Mojave and Yuma, from whom they were
separated by other tribal groups or by considerable distances
and formidable environments.

The first expedition of Europeans to come near the study
area was that led by Spanish army captain Juan Bautista de
Anza in 1774-1776. This expedition traveled across the Anza
Borrego Desert into Los Coyotes Canyon, and from there into
the Los Angeles Basin. By 1809 Cahuillas from the San Gorgonio Pass area, particularly from Whitewater Canyon, are
mentioned in Spanish mission records (Bean 1960). It is

apparent that from that time on, aspects of European culture spread rapidly among the Cahuilla, who of their own initiative seem to have left their home areas to learn such components of European culture as they wished to incorporate into their own culture. By 1819 an Asistencia was established at San Bernardino. The Cahuilla and Serrano were closely associated with it. Mission San Gabriel was grazing cattle as far as Palm Springs, in the study area, shortly thereafter (Bean and Mason 1962).

By this time some Cahuillas were already speaking Spanish in the Coachella Valley area, and had a keen political awareness of the ways of Spanish-Mexican culture. They began to develop new political and economic strategies with which to deal with the Spanish. They strengthened themselves politically by confederating several clans or remnants of former clans under one leader by the 1840s. Juan Antonio, Antonio Garra, and Chief Cabezon of the desert were among the important leaders who led such confederations. The new political strategies ensured the Cahuilla of considerable political control of their area well into the American period. As late as 1860 the Cahuilla outnumbered the Euroamericans in the area. According to the census of that year only 154 people out of a total of 2614 were not Indian. The Cahuilla were clearly in control of most of the area. The situation changed after a smallpox epidemic in 1863 destroyed large numbers of the Cahuilla. At the same time there was an influx of non-Indians into the area as emigrants arrived from the eastern

United States and elsewhere (U.S. Census 1860; Phillips 1975; Bean 1972).

Conditions rapidly became worse for the Cahuilla. Their population was decreasing and they were losing many of their traditional lands to outsiders. Their situation became so desperate that it attracted national attention. Investigations of conditions among the Cahuilla and other southern California Indians, and the desire of non-Indian newcomers to stabilize and/or remove Indians from areas which they wished to occupy or use as rangeland led by 1877 to the establishment of Indian reservations throughout the area. These included what is now Morongo Reservation (originally called Potrero, and then Malki), Torres-Martinez Reservation, Los Coyotes Reservation, Santa Rosa Reservation, Agua Caliente Reservation and others. Governmental interference in Indian affairs was at first rather slight, but by 1891 the government had established firm political and economic control over most reservations in the area. Nonetheless, traditional leadership patterns persisted, and much of the traditional religious and political system was intact. Cahuilla were still using many of their traditional hunting and gathering areas. As time went on, they began to rely less upon their traditional subsistence techniques, and became more intensively involved in stock raising, agriculture, and wage labor. By the late 1920s many of the Cahuilla were successfully participating in the American economic system. At this time most Cahuillas were resident members of various reservations. These reservations had established their own quite separate socio-cultural system. This system was not unlike that of the older ritual congregation. Various reservations cooperated regularly in socio-economic and religious activities which provided substantial economic and political benefits to all the Indian groups in the area. Much of the traditional political structure remained, and many traditional rituals were still practiced (Bean 1978).

In the 1930s the great American Depression affected the Cahuillas along with everyone else. Many Cahuillas who still remembered traditional hunting and gathering practices put them to good use during this time to alleviate economic stresses. The resurgence of such traditional practices during the Depression seems to have been an important factor in the maintenance of Cahuilla knowledge of their original territory and the use of its resources for human subsistence (Bean field notes).

World War II and changing economic conditions for small farmers, a drought, and many other factors acted in the other direction, contributing to a decrease of Cahuilla interest in traditional ways as well as a decrease in the exposure of non-Indians to these ways. Many young men served in the military forces. Others left the reservation for war-related jobs.

Fortunately, from the latter part of the 19th century until the 1930s, several anthropologists had visited the area, and collected valuable data about the Cahuilla while Cahuilla who remembered the old ways were still alive. David Prescott Barrows worked among them in the 1890s, publishing as a result an ethnobotany of the Cahuilla which has become a minor classic (Barrows 1900). A. L. Kroeber worked among the Cahuilla early in the 20th century (Kroeber 1907), E. W. Gifford (1918) came just before World War I, and Lucille Hooper (1920) came shortly afterward. William Duncan Strong (1929) and Philip Drucker (1937) followed. Some years later John Peabody Harrington collected information about the Cahuilla (Walsh 1976). After Harrington left, little work was done on the ethnography of the Cahuillas until Lowell John Bean began to work intensively with them in 1959 (Bean 1960; 1972; field notes, ca. 1960).

It is unfortunate that more work was not done, and that so few of the anthropologists who worked with the Cahuilla were interested in reconstructing the precise patterns of traditional land use and occupancy patterns, because we must now rely on intensive archaeological research to fill in the gaps in our knowledge about how the Cahuilla area was used. Cahuilla in the early part of this century would still have remembered many of these patterns. This is not to say that ethnographic knowledge is not still available, but that it is more difficult to acquire. Another factor that has inhibited data collection in the Cahuilla area is that much of the study area comprises lands which either were not intensively used after the establishment of reservations, or were not used by Cahuilla who were visited by field ethnographers. Moreover, even when Cahuillas were using some of this area for hunting and gathering and sacred purposes, they often kept the fact

secret from investigators in order to discourage relic hunters
and non-Indian hunters of game, and of course to preserve
their own sense of ethnic identity. It is only in recent
years, when the Cahuilla can see that much of this traditional
territory is vulnerable to further Euroamerican intrusion,
such as that posed by transmission lines, highways, and recreational uses, that they are taking more active interest in
recording data on the traditional use patterns of some of
their area.

Settlement Pattern

The southeastern part of the primary study area was a
major location for Cahuilla Indian settlement at various
periods. It is probable that about a thousand years ago the
freshwater Lake Cahuilla was about a hundred miles long, occu-
pying the basin now occupied by the Salton Sea. Some of the
Cahuilla developed a lacustrine economy and lived especially
along the western and northern shores of the lake. The Colorado River, which fed into it at that time, changed its course
about 500 years ago and no longer brought in water. The lake
began to fall when the water lost by evaporation was no longer
being replenished. As it fell the Cahuilla moved their villages and changed their patterns of subsistence to meet the
changed circumstances (Wilke 1976). In each period the Santa
Rosa Mountain range was an extremely attractive environment
for them, providing them with the flora and fauna of both the
lower, warmer elevations and the higher and cooler ones. In

contrast, the northwestern part of the study area has always been less desirable and less attractive. Fewer lineages are associated with this area, although a few of the Cahuillas living in the Coachella Valley did come from the mountain ranges to the east of that valley in the northwestern secondary study area rather than from the Santa Rosa range.

Cahuilla villages were generally located in or near the mouth of a canyon or in a valley. They were set up from the floors of canyons and valleys on one side or the other in order to avoid the significant water run-off coming down the canyons during certain periods. Despite this precaution, flash floods that destroyed entire villages are recorded in Cahuilla oral history. The siting of villages off the canyon or valley floors also placed them in the pathway of mountain breezes, which made the living sites more comfortable most of the year. A more significant fact is that these village sites were usually within an optimum distance from various plant and animal food resources at both low and high altitudes. Bean has suggested that most villages whose locations are known had approximately 80 percent of the food resources that people used the year around within a five mile radius (1972: 73-74). Elevations above 5000 feet in most of the Cahuilla area are relatively rare. Places at such heights were used occasionally for specific hunting and gathering activities. Snow and inclement weather, of course, prevented people settling permanently at these heights inasmuch as there were more attractive places for people to settle. In some

instances the Cahuilla did have winter and summer settlements.
We have been told by older Cahuilla informants that in such
places as Rock House Canyon people would move from village
sites at high elevations such as Old Santa Rosa village down
to the area of Hidden Spring, Ataki, during the colder months
to enjoy the warmer climate and to collect the plant foods
available there (Bean field notes, ca. 1960). Patencio mentions a similar movement among the people in the Palm Springs
area.

As of 1979 it is necessary to rely on data collected in
earlier years in order to establish in any detail what Cahuilla
settlement patterns were before contact. Even when William
Duncan Strong worked with them in the 1920s, Cahuilla had
moved around a great deal and it was difficult to establish
where some of their homes had been at any great distance into
the past. Fortunately, Cahuilla oral literature recounts some
of the movement of individual lineages in the various clans so
that a general pattern over time can be discerned. We see
that Cahuillas moved about in response to climatic changes,
because of pressures and opportunities derived from Euroamericans, and the effects of epidemic diseases introduced by
European populations. Within the study area there was a movement from the areas of Santa Rosa and Los Coyotes Canyons
eastward. Some of the people in Los Coyotes Canyon moved to
Rock House Canyon in the middle or late 19th century. Many
of the people who had lived in the Santa Rosa area became
followers of Juan Antonio (Costakik lineage), and moved into

the San Timoteo area or the San Gorgonio Pass area. Others moved from the Santa Rosa area out into the Colorado Desert and into the Coachella Valley. The people who moved from Los Coyotes Canyon to Santa Rosa village in Rock House Canyon apparently amalgamated to some degree with the Cahuillas of the original clan of that village. They lived there until the late 19th century when most of them moved to the present Santa Rosa Indian Reservation. This move was apparently made because the Cahuilla were beginning to move out more into American society and the reservation provided them with a guaranteed land base, and easier access to jobs and materials they needed to supplement their subsistence.

Other Cahuilla moved a shorter distance into Coachella Valley from villages in Toro Canyon, Martinez Canyon, and other canyons on the desert side of the Santa Rosa Mountains. These people maintained hunting and gathering privileges in the areas where they had previously lived, as did those who left Los Coyotes and Rock House Canyon villages. These traditional hunting and gathering rights were gradually eroded by time and distance. The final coup de grace to traditional land use patterns came in the 1890s with the full development of the reservation system. Indian agents and school teachers came in, children were put in Catholic or government boarding schools, and plans for economic development on reservations began to be implemented. Of course, there was an increasing hostility on the part of the invading non-Indians toward the idea of Indians using or encroaching upon any lands that were not

federally mandated Indian reserves. Descriptions of what
happened to Native American economic systems in southern
California during and after this period can be found in
Bean's discussion of what happened at Morongo reservation
(1978) and in Florence Shipek's Ph.D. dissertation (1977).

Springs, Streams and Wells

In an area where rainfall is as low as it is in the
study area, settlements must be placed where there is a
dependable water supply. In some places in the desert where
ground water was relatively close to the surface, the Cahuilla
dug walk-in wells to supply their water needs. In most places
they were dependent on either springs or year-round streams.
Mesquite groves and palm oases developed where there was water
close to the surface. Canyons such as Palm, Andreas, and
Murray had year-round streams. Many mountain areas in the
Santa Rosa Mountains had springs. It can be assumed that
spring sites were places known to the Cahuilla and used by
them, and that there were villages or significant use sites
near all major springs.

The Naming of Sites

Some Cahuillas state that all places were given names by
the Cahuilla. This, as with plant taxonomies, implies useful
or significant places. In the case of plants, many of little
or no use were identified under some generic term implying
that they were of little or no significance. They exhibited

a strong concern for naming places throughout the area and
developed a sophisticated taxonomic system for geographical
features which could precisely describe a geographic phenomenon. One of the reasons given for this was that having names
or precise designations for most places made it easier for
hunters or gatherers to know where they were so that they could
return themselves or send out other people to an area where a
kill had been made or a botanical or mineral resource found.
The hunter or collector could leave whatever game or other
resource he could not or did not carry home, and anyone he
sent out could find it without any difficulty (Bean field
notes).

In addition to names for specific places, the Cahuilla
had generalized place names. For example, the word for
dividing line or boundary was Keywatwahhewena (Patencio 1971:
56-57). According to Alice Lopez, the word for a place to
camp for the night, as in "I am going to sleep here tonight"
was tuka; a place where no one lives, an uninhabited or wild
area, was called iikinga; a place where you sit down, a tem-
porary place, was called chemmachvayika; and the name for a
place where people live was pachemkalivay. The term hemki
generally meant home, a place where people live, and the term
pahemnach meant people traveling around.

The Cahuillas tended to name every spring, conspicuous
rock, major outcrop of rock, canyon, grove, or other geographic
manifestations in their area. Place names often translate
into terms describing the environment, such as "near the

mouth," "in a canyon," "by the spring," "place of the acorn
trees," "place of the palm trees," "place of grass seeds,"
and so on. One village even had a name referring to the fact
that there was cracked earth there--the San Andreas fault
passed through it. One clan's name translates "touched by
the river," a name which suggests that the clan came from a
place which had experienced a flash flood.

Giving names to all parts of the environment is consistent with the general Cahuilla view of the world, which holds
that humans, plants, animals, and all other natural elements
were merged into one single consistent and interdependent
whole, and that often these independent parts are reservoirs
of residual "power" or symbolic representations of personages
of the Cahuilla creation time that could still affect the
daily lives of people (Bean 1976).

Oral Literature

Many of the features in Cahuilla ethnogeography are
explained in Cahuilla myths and legends. Cahuilla oral literature has not been as extensively recorded as one might hope,
nor has linguistic investigation been complete, so we will
probably never have the complete semantic domain of that sub-
ject that resided in the minds of tribal historians in the
past. However, what has been recorded, such as that by Patencio (1943; 1971), Gifford (1918), Kroeber (1908; 1925), and
Seiler (1970) does give us a strong indication of the detail
with which physiographic features were recorded. For example,

rock indentations left by nukatem, in illo tempore, that is, creation time, where cultural heroes walked or leaned or sat are mentioned. It is generally thought by Cahuillas that every adult Cahuilla knew with considerable precision the areas which belonged to him or were used by his family, his lineage, and even his clan. Certainly they knew where tribal group boundaries were, and knew a considerable amount of anecdotal material, both historic and mythic, about each of these places. The older Cahuillas interviewed in the 1960s took considerable pride about the detail with which they could remember geographic features and names of many of them. These names served as devices for stimulating traditional stories about Cahuilla culture and history.

CENTERS OF OCCUPATION

Several areas in the study area were centers of occupation and must be discussed in some detail because of the great concern that Cahuillas have for these areas.

The Santa Rosa and Rock House Canyon Areas

The area of Santa Rosa Indian Reservation, Nicholias (Nicolas) Canyon, and Rock House Canyon on the southwestern slopes of the Santa Rosa Mountains is not only of considerable cultural and historic importance to scholars, but also has special significance to contemporary Cahuillas. Since the

late 1950s the people on the Santa Rosa Reservation have been
outspokenly sensitive to any expression of interest by
non-Indians toward the reservation lands or nearby areas
remembered as Cahuilla territory in the past, especially the
village site called "Old Rock House." They have refused on
several occasions to cooperate with archaeologists who have
wanted to work in the area. However, unfortunately for Native
Americans and scholars, the area has been exploited by relic
collectors for many years, and many private and public collec-
tions contain items collected in this area. Even so, the
area is sufficiently intact that significant data could be
expected from a carefully conducted ethno-archaeological
study.

The area's occupation by Native Americans appears to be
confirmed by oral history. According to accounts provided by
Captain Poncho Lomas in the second decade of this century, the
Cahuilla came first from the east to an area west of the San
Jacinto Mountains. Later they moved across the San Jacintos
into the desert area at Martinez, northwest of the present
Salton Sea. This area, where the water table was relatively
high, provided abundant subsistence resources. When Lake
Cahuilla rose in the Salton Basin the Cahuilla ascended Martinez Canyon, and settled down in the village of Santa Rosa,
where they developed a rich lacustrine economy. When the
waters fell, the Cahuilla returned to the valley (G. W. James
1918:239-240). This general account has been reported to us
by other Cahuillas.

Strong says that there were roughly two groups of Mountain Cahuilla in the southern Santa Rosa mountain areas in late aboriginal times, one group centered in Coyote Canyon and one in the Santa Rosa Canyon area. The latter area included both Old and New Santa Rosa and the village of natcūta in Horse Canyon (1929:144-147). "...at Old Santa Rosa, which is situated in a fork of Rock House Canyon, were two villages, kolwovakut and kēwel, and at 'new' Santa Rosa was the village of sēwīu. Several miles to the northwest was the old town of natcūta, about one-half mile east of Horse Canyon" (1929:146).

The costakiktum lived at sēwīu, Santa Rosa, just south of Santa Rosa Mountain, Site 60. In 1846 the costakiktum, under the leadership of Juan Antonio, moved to Jurupa near Riverside and then to the San Timoteo Canyon (Strong 1929:145-151). Sēwīu is perhaps the site Reed is referring to when he says a branch of the trail from Nicolas Canyon to Santa Rosa Reservation leads to a village site where there used to be several Indian ollas until collectors found them and stole them (1963: 126).

Alice Lopez remembers going with her husband, Salvador Lopez, to the village of sēwīu. She says there was still an old house there, and apple and pear trees (Vane field notes, 1979). It was not possible to determine whether the site she visited was Site 60 or the Vandeventer Flat village, Site 223.

Immediately to the west of the costakiktum were the natcūtakiktum at natcūta in Horse Canyon, Site 116. Members of this clan also left the area under the leadership of Juan

Antonio. Tomas Arenas was net of this clan in about 1850, one of four nets among the northern Cahuilla clans. In the 1860s four families of this clan, members of the Arenas family, lived at sēupa on the Cahuilla reservation. In the 1920s two families, descended from one of these, were still extant (Strong 1929:145-157).

Five lineages of the wīwaīistam clan lived in the Coyote Canyon area. One of these, the sauicpakiktum, lived in Thousand Palm Canyon, off Collins Valley. After Juan Antonio led his group out of the Santa Rosa area, the sauicpakiktum segmented and the two resulting lineages occupied sēwia, "new" Santa Rosa, and kēwel, in Rock House Canyon, probably Site 27 (Strong 1929:145,148,151,158).

"New" Santa Rosa village, Site 60, is sometimes called we-wut-now-hu (Barrows 1900:37; Kroeber 1925:694). Barrows notes, "Returning to the mountains once more, among the rocks and pines on the south side of the isolated summit of Torres is a rough little valley, traversed by a small, rapid stream, to which the Indians long ago penetrated. Here is the interesting village of Santa Rosa, We-wut-now-hu ('pines'). These Indians make their homes during the winter months in the Coyote Canyon, a wide, sandy arm of the desert, thrust in south of Torres. Across this valley is the Coyote range of mountains. Up the sides of these mountains the Coahuillas found their way and established themselves in a beautiful and remote little glade, now known as the San Ignacio (Pa-cha-wal)" (Barrows 1900:34).

Early in the century George Wharton James reported,
"We are aiming for the Indian village of Santa Rosa, perched
high on the mountain of the same name" (1918:442). That would
be presently the Santa Rosa Reservation. It was the Vandeventer
Ranch. "Mr. Vandeventer tells us of the days when the Indians
lived by the hundreds in the nearby valleys. But as civiliza-
tion has crept closer to them they have mostly disappeared,
smallpox and consumption having aided the vices of the white
man in furthering their annihilation" (G. W. James 1918:443).

According to Al Benson, a prospector born at Fort Yuma
in 1868 and interviewed by Smith (1942:112), the Cahuilla said
that they were "driven into Rock House Canyon by Indian wars."
It is difficult to interpret information of this kind. The
Cahuillas to whom Benson referred may have been talking about a
pre-European conflict (Romero 1954) that drove their predeces-
sors into the valley, or about the conflicts of the 1850s in
the midst of which they themselves had moved to the canyon.
These included the Garra revolt in which a confederation of
Yuman-speakers from the Colorado River area and other southern
California Indians under the leadership of Antonio Garra united
against the vastly outnumbered Euroamericans in 1851, and were
vanquished only by the combined military forces of the United
States and Cahuillas led by Costakik leader Juan Antonio. The
leaders, including Antonio Garra, were caught in Los Coyotes
Canyon and subsequently executed (Strong 1929:185,250; Phillips
1975).

In Rock House Valley the Cahuilla built their houses of

rock piled up to about three feet and roofed with juniper branches and brush. Some were round, and some, possibly built after
contact with Mexicans, were square. Apparently priests from
San Ignacio "Mission" at San Ignacio Rancho had a subsidiary
mission in the canyon, coming there about once a month. The
mission was built in the same style as the houses. Prospector
Al Benson told Desmond Smith he remembered attending services
there with his father when he was seven years old--about 1875
(Smith 1942:112-113).

Benson described the place where the Cahuilla cremated the
dead. Two large slabs of rock were set on edge on either side
of a pit in which a fire was built. There was a drawing of
a man with outstretched arms on one rock. The ashes and remains
were placed in ollas which were buried in the cemetery below
the mission building. Benson said there remained none of these
which had not been broken by land movement in the vicinity.
Smith had heard an unconfirmed rumore that someone had taken
thirty crematory ollas from side canyons in the area (Smith
1942:112-113).

There was a severe smallpox epidemic in about 1875. Afterward there was a great deal of moving, as people fled homes
where relatives had died. It may have been at this time that
some sauicpakiktum people left Rock House Valley for the Torres-
Martinez area, e.g., the wantciñakik-tamianawitcem who went to
tūva (Strong 1929:41), and that other people came to take their
place. So many people died that whole lineages and clans became
extinct or nearly extinct. Apparently some marriages that

violated traditional rules took place at this time, and occasionally 2 or more clans consolidated to make one ceremonial unit. In at least one instance a ceremonial leader sent his ceremonial shell money to the net of another clan, and buried the ceremonial bundle of his clan after a last mourning ceremony, a formal recognition that a lineage or clan was no longer extant (Strong 1929:152-163).

In the late 19th century local white pioneers stayed away from Rock House Valley, knowing they were not welcome there. One outsider who ignored advice not to go into the area had his horse killed and sustained a bullet wound in his leg. In 1906 a local prospector found two horses tied up in the valley without food or water. He let them loose, but told two friends who were going prospecting about them. They entered Rock House Valley from Hidden Spring up Rock House Canyon and camped near a lone cottonwood tree near water (probably near Site 5). Looking around, they found one dead horse and clothing and camping equipment. A blanket had blood on it and two utensils had bullet holes in them. The next day, while panning for gold, one of them "looked up on the side of the hill, and there stood an old Indian with a 30-30 rifle on his shoulder and carrying a forked stick in the other hand.... After talking with the old fellow for awhile, they invited him to their camp and asked him to eat with them. The Indian accepted the invitation, but would not take any of the food until he had seen them eat some of it." He told them there was gold in abundance to the south, apparently in an effort to discourage them from staying in the valley. Making inquiries subsequently in the Coachella Valley, they learned at Mecca "that two men had walked out of Rockhouse saying their horses had been poisoned, and had then taken a train for Imperial Valley" (Reed 1963:72-74; 127). There are other accounts of Cahuillas protecting their area at this late date.

In 1909, Wayland Smith, in a Sequoyah League publication, reported, "The Santa Rosa Indians have asked for and are to receive their old home at Van De Venter Flat, called by them Se'-o-ya, pleasant view. Land has been reserved for them here, and water sufficient for present needs appropriated" (Smith 1909).

Rock House Valley contains the ruins of several villages, spectacular as California archaeological sites go because they contain the ruins of the rockwalled houses. Site 16 is known as "Old Santa Rosa" (U.S. War Department, U.S. Army, Corps of Engineers 1944). It is not possible to say who occupied this site and when without further investigation. It is well served by trails, and was probably one of the villages occupied by people in the "northern" group, related to the costakiktum and wīwaīistam in the late precontact period (Strong 1929: 146-148). It was occupied during the latter part of the 19th century by the sauicpakiktum who had moved there earlier from the Los Coyotes area.

Site 27 is apparently the site investigated in 1953 by a field team from the San Diego Museum of Man. It has been assumed to be kēwil (Strong 1929:146) and may be.

Reed says that "portions of the rock walls of the Tortes home are still to be seen in the southern portion of Rockhouse Valley where there are the remains of three other rockhouses-- one of them the home of the Andreas family" (1963:122). The Tortes and Andreas families were the last members of the sauicpakiktum to live in the valley. Reed goes on to say that half a mile east of the Tortes rockhouse was a watering place near a cottonwood tree from which the Tortes and Andreas families probably obtained their water--perhaps Cottonwood "spring" (Reed says it was not really a spring, but a place where the water was close to the surface). "At the base of Toro Peak, in the northern portion of Rockhouse Valley, near a little spring of water are the remains of another rockhouse Indian village.... To the south of the little spring is a rock circle that is still very much intact, and even though this wall is circular instead of being made with four corners as all the others were, it no doubt was one of their dwelling places." Reed also describes the ruins of another rectangular dwelling place and says that there are other places without rock walls that appear to have been house sites (Reed 1963:122-123). It would appear that the site at the base of Toro Peak was Site 16, Old Santa Rosa, and that the Toro and Andreas families lived at Site 27.

Calistro Tortes was the last Cahuilla to live in Rock House Valley. He was the son of Manuel Tortes, "chief of the Rockhouse Valley Indians" (Reed 1963:122), and brother of Celestin Tortes, who was David Prescott Barrows' principal guide on his

research trips in the Cahuilla area. Calistro was born sometime between 1860 and 1880 and lived into the 1960s. According
to Bean's field notes, he was the last of the Cahuillas living
then who had lived at Old Santa Rosa. Reed says that he was
born at Hidden Springs (1963:120), in the village of Ataki.
Juan Siva identified the Hidden Spring village as Ataki (Bean
field notes, ca. 1960). Strong says that this was the place
from which the three desert Cahuilla clans, the watciñakiktum,
palpunivikiktum, and watcinakik-tamīanawitcem clans, originally
came. The first two of these later lived at Puīchekiva near
Martinez, and the third at tūva (Strong 1929:41). The residents of Rock House Valley are said to have come down to the
Hidden Spring area in winter to take advantage of its warmer
climate and winter vegetation and hunting opportunities (Bean
field notes, ca. 1960).

Ataki was on a mesa above a hidden spring. It is probable
that there were both early and late occupations here. Some
house pits were distinguishable in the 1930s. An amateur
archaeologist from El Cajon dug out burials here in the 1930s.
All had Caucasian material in them. One skull had a bandana
handkerchief about the head (Anonymous, ca. 1938).

Merriam's notes contain several references to the Santa
Rosa/Rock House Valley people. According to him, the Pow'-we-
yam clan occupied the west slope of the San Jacinto Mountains
south of Latitude 33 40'. These were the western neighbors of
the Sow'-wah-pah-keek-tem people who were the "Santa Rosa
Mountain tribe." To the north were the Wah'-ki-chi'-m-kut-tem

(also spelled Sow-wis-pan-kik-tem or Sauispakiktum) at Vandeventer Flat at a later date and gives the village there the
Cahuilla name sa-we-ah or seu-yah. He says the original name
was sowis-is-pakh. Such naming is typical in Cahuilla (Field
notes: X/2300-11/G57). This is the lineage name of the Tortes
family. In Cahuilla the word sawish refers to a flat bread-
cake made from acorn meal and water. The family subsequently
took the name Tortes, from the Spanish "tortilla," for their
family name.

Strong did not locate "new" Santa Rosa at Vandeventer
Flat (1929:145), and it would appear that the village there may
have been named sa-we-ah after the sauispakiktum moved "back"
there in 1909 (Smith 1909).

Rock House Canyon is mentioned frequently in Cahuilla oral
literature. In a migration myth recounted to Hansjacob Seiler
by Joe Lomas in 1964, ancestors of the Cahuilla at Torres, led
by the hero Yellow Body, traveled from Rock House Canyon to
where the Torres Reservation is now located, and from there to
Cupa Hot Springs (Warner Hot Springs), where they entered the
water, to live on as immortal brown dogs (Seiler 1970:64-73).
Patencio says that Yellow Body settled for a time at Deep
Canyon. At the same time another culture hero named Mul li kik
settled at Vandeventer Flat (Site 89), which was called San we
yet. Yellow Body sent his dog to the people at San we yet to
choose a family for Yellow Body's sister to marry into. The
dog passed by the houses of those who tried to entice him to
come to them, and went to the last house, where they fed him.

The dog having reported favorably on the householders, Yellow Body sent his sister to marry into that family (Patencio 1943: 37-38).

The trail between Santa Rosa Reservation and Rock House Valley leads through Nicholias (sometimes spelled "Nicolas") Canyon. This trail passes Nicolas Spring, the source of the stream which has cut the canyon. "On a ridge to the south and east of the spring, are the remains of the old Nicolas rockhouse, and in a basin to the north and east of the site is a row of cottonwood trees that were no doubt planted by the Indians. Along the side of the hill below the spring is evidence of a ditch through which the Indians probably ran water from the spring to water their garden" (Reed 1963: 122-125).

Nicolas Spring and Canyon were named after Nicolas Guanche, the last of the Guanche family to live there. He died an old man between 1914 and 1921. Members of the Guanche family still live at Santa Rosa Reservation. There are metates and weathered pictographs on the boulders to the west of the stream, suggesting that the canyon has been used for hundreds of years. Nicolas Spring, Canyon, and village comprise Site 203 (1963:123-126).

The peak of Santa Rosa Mountain (Site 84) is considered sacred by the Cahuilla. It is typical of the Cahuilla cosmological tradition, as of many other traditions, to consider such places sacred. It is associated with seeing "high" and distant and remote places as the homes of sacred beings or the places where they touch down when they visit "middle earth." This peak, like Tahquitz Peak, also in Cahuilla territory, is such a place. Sacred persons, such as Cahuilla net'em (lineage or clan administrators) or puvulum (shamans) frequently visited such places to receive inspiration and power. The Cahuilla, according to Patencio, called the Santa Rosa mountain weal um mo. The culture hero Yellow Body rested there to remove a troublesome cholla cactus thorn from his foot. He threw a thorn on a top of a large rock, where it grew, and named the mountain weal um mo (Patencio 1943:38). Bean's field notes indicate that the mountain was called sen villet (Bean, ca. 1960). Barrows recorded the name Cawish wa-wat-acha, or the "mighty mountain" (Barrows archival notes, ca. 1897-1899).

A ridge of the mountain was reportedly named Hiawat (Chase 1919). This is Site 275.

There is a petroglyph site, Site 46, located at the upper end of the east fork of Rock House Canyon, and about a mile south of Site C-146 (about which there is no data beyond this reference and that noted under Site 42 and 43T). The petroglyphs are on the east face of a large granite boulder. A few sherds were found at the site. The site report from which these data are drawn is included in the Appendix, Site C-136 (Anonymous, ca. 1938). Steward (1929:95) and others have described pictograph/petroglyphs to the east of this, Riv-15. They may be the same as Site 46. They were sketched by E. N. Wear, who wrote of them, "The drawings

do not show all of the cuttings or incised work as it is
quite impossible to follow it in all detail. This is on a
very smooth surface that...faces the north."

Within a mile of the secondary study area is a village
site, Site 15, which lies on a trail that follows Coyote
Flat to Vandeventer Flat (Strong 1929:146-148).

Meighan surveyed sites in Rock House Canyon, Collins
Valley, Indian Canyon, Coyote Creek, and Clark Dry Lake in
the late 1950s (1959). One hundred seventy-three sites were
discovered which dated to about A.D. 1000. He pointed out
that an enormous amount of looting of archaeological material had taken place, perhaps the most anywhere in California.
He indicated that sites even in the most remote and inaccessi-
ble parts of the Borrego Park suffered from the collecting
and digging of vandals. Most sites consist mostly of surface
remains. In some, these had been picked over intensively
and only a few small potsherds were found which would war-
rant further investigation or excavation. Active digging was
going on by relic collectors during the time of his survey.
Other archaeologists since that time have noted that continu-
ing vandalism and damage from recreational vehicles are significant destroyers of archaeological or historic evidence
in this area.

Palm Springs Area

The entire area around Palm Springs is close to the
hearts of Native Americans who live there now or whose

ancestors lived there. It is highly sensitive to them because of cultural and historical reasons. The sensitivity has been heightened conflict between Indians and non-Indians over land use rights in the area for several generations. Participation in legal suits against federal and local governing bodies regarding land use has long been part of the day-to-day existence of the Agua Caliente Cahuilla of Palm Springs. Attempts to acquire or control the use of land owned by the Agua Caliente band of Cahuilla Indians by speculators, environmentalists, the city of Palm Springs and others have been vigorous. The long-continuing conflict between Native Americans and others over land use is exacerbated by prejudicial feelings toward Indians common among non-Indians of the area. They commonly express resentment that Indians have a controlling interest in much of the land in the area. Only rarely have mitigating actions been taken by public officials toward alleviating this condition.

Palm Springs developed around the now famous hot springs, known as the Agua Caliente Springs. These were also a center of Native American (Cahuilla) occupation and religious activity. There are numerous references in the literature to these springs, se'e in Cahuilla, Site 83, but these and other sites within the city are not within a mile of the study area and will not be discussed in any further detail. Our concern here will be with the several canyons south of Palm Springs which are within the study area. The largest of these is Palm Canyon.

Palm Canyon

This canyon was the home of the kauisiktum clan. Because kauisiktum leaders recorded much of their oral literature, there is a considerable amount of data about their traditional areas. Palm Canyon is conspicuous because of its splendid natural resources, inspiring suggestions that it be developed as a private or public recreational area, such as a National Park. Such suggestions exacerbate the sensitivity that many of the Agua Caliente Cahuilla have towards non-Indians who pressure them for uses of Indian land which are not directly related to their own needs.

Cahuilla oral history of the canyon includes the story of an early people who walked across the mountains to Palm Canyon from the area of the San Jacinto plain. One of their leaders turned himself into a rock and "he is there in the rock yet" (Patencio 1943:33). This is now one of the many "power" rocks in Cahuilla territory. Any large rock formation in the Cahuilla area is likely to be such a transformed personage, or a place of residual supernatural power from the Cahuilla "beginnings."

In another account the son of Ca wis ke on ca, an important culture hero, moved to Palm Canyon from a previous home (Patencio 1943:90). Another culture hero, Evon ga net, called a place in Palm Canyon Sim mo ta (Site 295), meaning "Indian corral or pasture." He also named a second place in the canyon Fat mel mo, meaning "a place among many hills" (Site 205). Unfortunately the exact location of these places cannot be specified with any confidence. A third place named by the culture hero can be located somewhat more specifically--Gash mo, meaning "the sound of crunching sand as one walks," said to be a place to the east side of the area once called the "Garden of Eden" (Site 297). (Patencio 1943:53).

The son of Ca wis ke on ca who moved to a place near Palm Canyon called the place Tev ing el we wy wen it, meaning "a round flat basket closed up at the top, that is hung up." Here he lived, and raised a large family. He had a ceremonial house here. A territory was given him by his brother--the land from "Idyllwild down to Palm Canyon, through the west side of the Murray Hills; then across to the Little Canyon of one Palm near the beginning of the Andreas Club Road, north on Andreas Canyon" (Patencio 1943:90). This may be the description of a lineage's territory, possibly the kauisiktum. It is designated Site 49. This canyon is mentioned in Cahuilla literature; for example, in several accounts which discuss conquest and warfare.

At a place that is now known as Indian Potrero, Palm Springs people of the early time are said to have beaten the heads of their Seven Palms enemies on a big rock after a battle between the Palm Springs people and the Seven Palms people. The name of the Place You koo hal ya me means "place of many brains" (Patencio 1943:89). This is Site 294. It appears that the Seven Palms people were displaced by the group that came from the San Jacinto plain area. The presence of petroglyphs in the area signifies the territorial claims of one group over the other.

In another Cahuilla source, William Pablo, Wanakik leader, recalls that in 1825 a terrible epidemic of small-pox threatened the Cahuilla people. Indian doctors, he reports, held a council to decide how to treat the disease. The meeting took place in Palm Canyon. In this account the name of Palm Canyon is said to have been "Taquitz." An error of some sort has possibly come through in the translation. This rather lengthy account points out that "paintings and hieroglyphics are found in our Indian caves," which interpret or tell what happened to these caves. Other local personages mentioned in this account include Chief Andres Lucero, presumably of the Andreas family (Panikiktum lineage). Sick people were sent to a cave in Chino Canyon to receive treatment and be "rendered immune" to the disease (Romero 1954:2-4).

Melba Bennett, a resident of Palm Springs for many years, notes that in 1885 an Indian village was located in Palm Canyon about three miles south of Palm Springs in the extreme southwest corner of Section 35. The home of the "chief" was on the west side of the road to Rincon, and the other houses were situated across the road (Bennett field notes 1948). The site of this village is Site 18.

At the mouth of Palm Canyon there is a flat rock with mortar holes. The place was called tevin' imulwiwaīwinut (Strong 1929:100). Such places were used for grinding various plant foods by Cahuilla women. They were usually owned by individuals or families (Bean 1972). It is Site 220.

Merriam (Field notes; date unknown) says that Palm Canyon was the boundary between two Cahuilla linguistic groups. He interviewed Cahuilla about place names and was given the following data:

The paniktem occupied the lower end of Palm Canyon between the Kavisik and the Wak-ko-chim. In another note he says that the paniktum were a tribe who occupied the middle part of Palm Canyon, including Murray and West canyons. In still another note he says the paniktem were "over" Palm Canyon, west to Andreas Canyon and up to West Fork Canyon. There was a group called the kutam, one of the kavic group.

Merriam also notes that the wak-ko-chim-kut-em was a "tribe" in the upper part of Palm Canyon--17 miles according to one note--reaching southerly and easterly over Haystack and Asbestos mountains, and Pinyon Flat to the south side of the Santa Rosa mountains (Merriam field notes, undated).

In another place he says that the Wah-ko-chimut were around the West Fork to Vandeventer Flat to the base of the Santa Rosa mountains, and down each side of Palm Canyon to opposite West Fork again southeast of the Indian Wells tribe.

Elsewhere he says, "Adjoining the Wah'-ne-ke'-tem [Mahl-ke] on the southeast are the Kah'-wis-se-tum [Kauisiktum] or Palm Springs (Agua Caliente No. 2) tribe, which begins at the point of the mountain near Whitewater Station and reaches easterly to a huge elongate sand dune (over a rocky base) called Yah'-wah-kis; and thence southerly to the mouth of

Palm Canyon; across this to the west and up the north rim
of San Andreas Canyon to Eagle Cliff at the summit; thence
northerly around the head of Tahquitz Canyon and San Jacinto
Peak and down the ridge to the place of beginning near
Whitewater Station.

"Adjoining the Kah'-wis-se-tem on the south are the
Pahn-vik-tem or Palm Canyon people (paniktum). Their territory embraces Palm Canyon and the adjacent mountain slopes
on the west from the north side of Andreas Canyon to West Fork
Canyon.

"Adjoining the Pahn-vik-tem on the south were the
Wah-ke-chī'm-kut, now extinct, who extended southerly over
the upper reaches of Palm Canyon and adjacent slopes on both
sides from West Fork Canyon to beyond Vandeventer Flat and
on to the very base of Santa Rosa Mountain. They spoke the
same dialect as the Santa Rosa Mountain people.

"Adjoining the Wah-ke-chī'm-kut on the east were the
Kah-vi'-nish or Indian Wells tribe" (Merriam field notes, date
unknown).

Some descendants of the Serranos also have an interest
in Palm Canyon. The Serrano at Morongo Reservation were a
part of the ceremonial network (ritual congregation) of the
people in Palm Springs, as were the peoples at Cahuilla,
Santa Rosa, Torres-Martinez and several other reservations
of this area. All of these people intermarried, and so are
often closely related genealogically. It has been said that the

great great grandfather of Sarah Martin, past ceremonial leader of the Maringa Serrano, lived for a time in Palm Canyon (Bean field notes). Her great grandmother lived there with him and his wife.

One of the many archaeological features in Palm Canyon was witnessed by desert reporter Randall Henderson, who saw a series of Indian shrines, piles of pebbles and small rocks, spread along both sides of the trail up Palm Canyon at irregular intervals. At the time they were well preserved and quite conspicuous (Henderson 1941). These are at Site 157.

Palm Canyon stretches southward through the Santa Rosa mountains all the way to Vandeventer Flat. The trail through the canyon, Site 207, was an important link in a complex of trails over which people moved all over southern California. At Vandeventer Flat and elsewhere, it connected with trails that led to Pinyon Flat, Santa Rosa village, and westward to the coast (Patencio 1943:71; Jaeger 1953). The trail from the Palm Canyon trail to Asbestos Spring at the edge of Pinyon Flat is Site 28. It leads into Horse Potrero Canyon to Potrero Spring, Site 30, along the eastern slope of Asbestos Mountain to Asbestos Spring.

Springs are essential to travellers along any trail in this dry country. There were a number of these along the main trail in Palm Canyon. Just outside the primary study area was Agua Bonita Spring, Site 32, near Big Falls, famous to local travellers. Halfway up the canyon was a hot spring, Site 221. This spring was named Paskwa (means "mortars") by the culture hero, the "great net." It was associated with rock mortars (Strong 1929:100). The same net named the southern end of Palm Canyon Tatmĭlmĭ (1929:100), Site 222.

Hidden Falls, Site 155, is a well hidden scenic phenomenon, possibly over 50 feet high in Palm Canyon. This was very likely an important site to the Cahuilla, with ritual significance, but it is not mentioned in the ethnographic literature that we have searched (Henderson 1941). Hermit's Bench, Site 156, at the lower end of Palm Canyon, is one of many palm oases in the canyon (Henderson 1941:26).

Andreas Canyon

Andreas Canyon branches off from Palm Canyon near its mouth. It has cultural and historical significance to both Indians and non-Indians interested in the study area. Its great natural beauty and its cultural significance have drawn the attention of many of those who have been concerned with explaining the southern California desert's positive features to others, such as James (1908; 1918), Chase (1919), Saunders (1913; 1914), and Jaeger (1953).

Andreas Canyon is named after an important Cahuilla leader of the Paniktum lineage who had a home and agricultural lands there in historic times. There were agricultural fields here at an early date (Wilke and Lawton 1975:33). The territory of the Paniktum (Cahuilla), according to Merriam (Field notes, date unknown) was from the north side of Andreas Canyon to the West Fork of Palm Canyon.

Conspicuous archaeological features of the canyon include:

1) A pictograph site (Smith and Turner 1975:photos and plates 6,7; Patencio 1943:103). This is Site 216.

2) A large cave shelter consisting of an overhanging rock under which are bedrock mortars. This is referred to by local people as "Gossip Rock." Cahuillas have indicated that each grinding rock belonged to a particular family. Most of these were "washed" away before 1948. Various seeds (acorns, mesquite beans, palm dates) of indigenous plants as well as of domesticated plants were ground in these mortars (Bean field notes, ca. 1960).

3) Beneath the rock containing the petroglyph there is a rock with "saw teeth" which was used to draw hide through in order to make it pliable enough for carrying straps, thongs, and the like. This same sheltered area was used to chip arrowheads (Bean ca. 1960).

4) According to one Cahuilla elder, the pictographs on a rock at the mouth of Andreas Canyon depict the history of the Agua Caliente people, including the "legend of the Palo Verde tree." According to this legend, the great chief Tachevah's daughter was abducted by Tahquitz, disappearing at the mouth of Andreas Canyon, where later a Palo Verde tree grew to mark the spot (Klein, date unknown).

5) Andreas Canyon provided water from several sources for the Cahuilla people living at Rincon. In historic times they brought water in ditches from Andreas Canyon to the

groves of figs, grapes, oranges and other plants which they
cultivated. It is reported that they worked closely with
Dr. Welwood Murray, a pioneer of Palm Springs. Eventually
another developer diverted the water from the canyon to his
own development, called the "Garden of Eden." George Wharton
James (1918:294) recalls that Captain Andreas, who farmed
here, was a man of "considerable energy, who lived in an
adobe house. He had a vineyard and produced wine for local
distribution." It is possible that agriculture was practiced
in this area prior to European contact. The area may be of
considerable archaeological signficance consequently.

6) There are several groves of palm trees in the canyon.

7) The site of the village in Andreas Canyon is Site 125.

The condition of Andreas Canyon in the early part of the
century has been described by J. Smeaton Chase in his California Desert Trails (1919). He camped at the rock shelter
for several months while journeying throughout the southern
California deserts. The cavern (rock shelter) served as his
"dining room, study and kitchen." It was "adorned" by "picture writing." He says an "upper story was quite a museum of
age-dimmed records in red and black." He says that one up-
right stone was "worn into grooves like knuckles, where arrow shafts had been smoothed," and describes a stone that
"showed evidence of having been used for polishing the ob-
sidian points." He says a "dozen" bedrock mortars were there,
and that occasionally he "unearthed...deer-horn awls and
ornaments of shell and clay" and various bone materials of

different shapes (1919:20).

Jane Penn of Morongo Indian Reservation recalls visiting the canyon at about 1917. Some of the people were still using traditional houses for shelter, and waters were diverted from the stream to the houses for domestic use. Mrs. Penn's father, William Pablo, a well-known political and religious leader of the Wanikik, is said to have been born there. Andres Painik (Chief Andres) was his maternal grandfather. He was born about 1800 at Painik near Andreas Canyon (Curtis 1926:110, photo 2).

The Kauisiktum owned a portion of Andreas Canyon, too. According to Merriam (Field notes, date unknown) their territory "begins at the point of the mountain near Whitewater Station and reaches easterly to a hugh elongate sand dune (over a rocky base) called Yah-wah-kis; and thence southerly to the mouth of Palm Canyon; across this to the west and up the north rim of San Andreas Canyon to Eagle Cliff at the summit; thence northerly around the head of Tahquitz Canyon and San Jacinto Peak and down the ridge to the place of beginning near Whitewater Station."

Andreas Canyon also has historic import because Carl Eytel, a famous painter and illustrator, used features of the canyon for much of his art and because the famous pioneer ethnographer and photographer Edward Curtis used the canyon as background for some of his photographic studies of Indian culture.

Murray Canyon

This canyon opens into Palm Canyon somewhat to the south of the mouth of Andreas Canyon. It, also, is significant to the Cahuilla. The canyon and its environs are mentioned frequently in Cahuilla oral literature.

Francisco Patencio recalled that the Murray Hills are "full of trails," and that wild mountain sheep went to the top of Murray Peak at lambing time. Trails cross the Murray Hills from the "Garden of Eden," passing Eagle Spring on the way to Indian Wells, Magnesia Canyon, and Cathedral Canyon. These run back into Palm Canyon country, joining a trail network that goes to Pinyon Flats and other places of importance in the Santa Rosa Mountains (1971:16).

Murray Hill was called sewitckul, a name given it by the culture hero, the "great net" (Strong 1929:100). In a tale recorded by Patencio, the Murray Hills are called Wa wash ca le it, meaning "stripes on the hills . . . and the same stripes or streaks are there today." The name was given them by the Cahuilla culture hero Evon ga net (Patencio 1943:53).

Murray Canyon was called eīt, meaning "thief," by the "great net" (Strong 1929:100).

The area was rich in food resources. Throughout the spring and early summer water flows freely down this canyon. It is therefore rich in flora and fauna. Deer were commonly found near camps and mountain sheep at higher levels. Significant flora include palm trees, pinyon trees, yucca, many species of edible cacti, and other low shrubs common to the arid lands of southern California. These plants attract rodents and other animals which were used by the Cahuilla (Bean and Saubel 1972).

Martinez Canyon

Martinez Canyon was, prior to European contact, the home of the Wantcinakiktum lineage of the Wildcat moiety. The isilsiveyyaiutcem also occupied the area, but at another and later period of time. The wantcinakiktum originally came from Atakī (Hidden Spring in the lower portion of Rockhouse Canyon) (Strong 1929:41; Bean field notes, ca. 1960). The name "wantcinakiktum" also refers to a mountain in the Santa Rosas. Its exact location is not known.

The wantcinakiktum lived at the village of puīchekiva. When this village "broke up," they moved to Martinez Canyon and established a village called Īsilsīveyaiutcem (Site 204). Strong felt that this was the original home of the clan before they moved to the desert. Contemporary descendants of the lineage include the present-day Siva family, now for the most part associated with the Los Coyotes Reservation. Pablo Siva of the lineage was living at Martinez when Strong collected his data on the Cahuilla in the 1920s (1929:45).

When the wantcinakiktum clan moved to the desert, they shared living space with the awilem lineage, although they still had their own food gathering areas at Martinez Canyon where they went in the spring and early summer to gather cacti (1929:47). It was here that three families who had

lived at the village puīchekiva with the awilem went when
that village was abandoned (1929:47). Juan Siva recalled to
Bean (ca. 1960) that the Īsilsiva were at one time in the
desert, and then moved into the mountains at the edge of
Martinez, near Vallerie, and south of Rabbit Peak. The
Īsilsiva lived there, where there was a natural reservoir,
and went back and forth to Borrego, planting watermelons,
squash, corn, and beans. Juan Siva's grandfather said the
rabbits were eating the plants, so they built a cactus fence
of chukal to keep rabbits out. The rabbit fence is still
there in Collins Valley according to Katherine Siva Saubel.
In the summer they were in the mountains harvesting pinyons.
Afterward they went back to Borrego. After a while some of
the men didn't like it, ill feelings of some kind developed,
and so cloudbursts were sent to destroy the plantings. Rain
washed the plants away so people couldn't plant any more. The
Īsilsiva them moved to Wilyi in the Los Coyotes area. This
was in the early 1800s.

The Īsilsivas were wanchum before they were Īsilsivas.
They originally lived in the Santa Rosa mountains and are
closely related to the awilem. They moved from the Martinez
area because someone was killing their children (Bean ca. 1960).

Martinez Canyon was described by George Wharton James
(1918:239-240). He recalls that the canyon contained oco-
tilla, yucca whipplei, Opuntia and Echinocacti. He describes
an elevated mesa from which there is a spectacular view of
the desert.

James says that Captain Pancho Lomas told him that the people of Torres came into the desert over the San Jacinto mountains, although originally, "in the beginning," they came from the east. They travelled for a long time on their trip over the San Jacintos. They were naked and had little food, and had to subsist on what plants and animals they could find. When they came to Martinez, they found that people had dug wells, so that mesquite trees and other food plants grew in abundance. Game was plentiful in the nearby mountains. It was an attractive spot, so they settled down in content.

After they had lived there for a while, the waters rose in the Salton basin and drove them out of Martinez. They moved up Martinez Canyon, and finally to the village of Santa Rosa. The inland sea provided fish, which they caught with their stone fish traps, "rudely circular in shape...from two and one-half to nine feet in diameter, and give the impression they were built at low tide, so that as the water came in fish would enter and be caught" (James 1918:239-240). Wilke (1976) has demonstrated that the fish traps were built as the inland lake fell, causing fish to be plentiful on the shoreline. As the lake became too saline, the fish died.

James' informant also told him about the return to the desert when the water came down. "When the water first went down, the land had very little on it, only a few grasses, and the people did not have much to eat. Then the grasses grew more plentifully and soon the prickly pear and mesquite came and then all was well" (1918:239-240).

Toro Canyon Area

The Toro Canyon area was a major occupation area for the Cahuilla people in historic and prehistoric times. Today it is an area about which Cahuillas are concerned for cultural and historical reasons. The area contained a major village site, mauūlmiī (Place of the Palm Tree), evidence of deep water wells, an historic cemetery, various hunting and gathering areas, and the like.

It is said to have been the home of the sawalakiktum Cahuilla (Gifford 1918). Many other Cahuilla have used the canyon area in the past several generations. Most elderly or knowledgeable Cahuillas recall its use. The anthropological informants who have recalled it include Salvador Lopez, Juan Siva, Calistro Tortes, Alice Lopez, and Ruby Modesto. Gifford (1918), Merriam (field notes, date unknown), and Strong (1929: 52) agree that the wakaīkiktum clan lived here. Gifford says that this clan originally lived near Warner's ranch, but was not Cupeño. Their location was probably in the Los Coyotes Canyon area (1918:190). Strong says the wakaīkiktum originally lived at tcīuk "back in the Santa Rosa mountains, then at panūksī at the head of a canyon about seven miles south of Indio, and later came to mauūlmiī"(1929:52). According to Strong, the wakaīkiktum (night heron) and the pañakauissiktum (water fox) clans lived at mauūlmiī in about the 1870s. The former occupied ten houses, three of them communal, and the latter, six houses. They shared the well (actually there were at least 3 wells here), which was probably dug by the pañakau- issiktum as earliest residents. There were two ceremonial houses, and each clan had its own area where plants were cultivated, and its own gathering area, presumably throughout the canyon.

Apparently the sewahilem (mesquite that is not sweet) lineage also moved to mauulmii from near La Mesa about 1895 (1929:52). Gifford also says the tamolañitcem lineage, Wildcat moiety, lived at Toro, but he may have meant another place (1918:190).

Mauulmii is CSRI Site 23. We have also located "Toro Village" at Site 64. There are frequent references in the literature to Toro Village, but it is not clear whether this is always in reference to the village known to Cahuillas as mauulmii or there may at times be confusion with Torres, the location of the Torres Indian Reservation.

In one reference to Toro, Patencio tells of chiefs' calling a meeting in order to punish bad people. They are said to have gathered the warriors from Toro and Morongo, men from all tribes everywhere, and proceeded to Yucaipa to punish the malefactors--an indication that precontact Cahuilla Indians organized clans who lived some distance apart to go on the offensive (Patencio 1971).

With reference to a later period, Patencio says that the Pony Express ran through the desert via Palm Springs carrying the mail once a week between Yuma and San Bernardino, whence it was sent on to Los Angeles and San Francisco. The riders followed Indian trails, stopped where the Indians lived, and were supplied with food and water by the Indians, a fact confirmed by not only historical records, but also by Cahuilla oral tradition. One of the stops was El Toro, on the way from Martinez to Indian Wells. This was the same route taken by the Butterfield Trail, and later a country road (Johnston 1977).

Johnston says that the Toro area was heavily populated by Cahuillas in the 1850s and 1860s. "Cabezon lived here and more or less controlled his people from this point" (1977:120). There was a stop here for the Banning stage from an early period (1977:120).

The water supply at Toro came from wells dug by the Cahuilla. Several observers have commented on them (Site 39).

> The whole valley of the Cabeson (Coachella Valley) is dotted with wells, most of them marking sites of homes long ago abandoned, the wells themselves being now only pits partly filled with sand, but many dug in the old way still remain, supporting life, and giving refreshment miles and miles away from the rocky walls where the streams of the mountains disappear in the sands. These wells are usually great pits of terraced sides leading down to the narrow holes at the bottom where water sparkles, built in such a way that a woman with an olla on her head can walk to the water's edge and dip her painted vessel full. . . . There is no question but that the Cahuilla learned of themselves to dig these wells, and this practice cannot perhaps be paralleled elsewhere among the American Indians [Barrows 1900:26-27].

Baldwin says that there were then eight Indian wells on the Toro Reservation lying in a straight line about half a mile long. From them, trenches four to eight feet deep ran downward to clumps of mesquite trees which the wells irrigated. Not all the trenches, which ranged upward from 125 feet in length, were still intact. The wells in 1938 were no longer in use and did not contain water, but mesquite trees and other vegetation marked their location (Baldwin 1938).

A great many artifacts and features have been found at

the site of Toro village, including round and rectangular
house pits, tools of bone, stone, wood, and pottery. Some
of the bone artifacts are incised. There are pipe fragments,
bone awls, projectile points, scrapers and an enormous quan-
tity of pottery. The floor of a ceremonial house was evident
when Bean visited the site in 1960, as well as other house
floors. A number of cremations have also been found at the
site.

In the historical period people were buried in a cemetery
just within the study area at Site 36. Despite the fact that
it has been used in recent years, and in fact is still used,
it has suffered a great deal of damage from marauders,
pot hunters, and people who use the desert for recreation.

To the south of Toro are some of the fish traps which the
Cahuilla used, several hundred years ago, to catch fish at
the shores of Lake Cahuilla (Wilke 1976:178-180). These are
more completely discussed under Site 34 in Chapter III.

Near the fish traps are petroglyphs which are also very
significant for Cahuilla people. These are discussed under
Site 35 in Chapter III.

Whitewater Canyon

According to tradition, the Cahuilla culture hero, Evon
ga net, found desert willows growing along Whitewater Wash.
He called the place Con kish wi qual, which means "two desert
willows." Then he went south across the valley to where jagged
red rocks "still stand alone by the side of the highway." He
named these Kish chowl, "sharp pointed house roofs." Three

quarters of a mile along the Whitewater "ditch," he named a
large pile of rocks Lin Kish mo. "Going west along the valley, which is now the highway, he came to another point. This
he called Ta was ah mo, meaning a good view for hunting." Going
on, he called Whitewater Point Ta mare, meaning the mouth or
opening of a pass, crossed Snow Creek and named it Na hal log
wen et, "the center of an open place" (Patencio 1943:54).

Although these sites are apparently not in the study area,
they are part of the general area of Whitewater Canyon and
Whitewater Wash and adjacent Morongo Pass. Their inclusion
in the story of Evon ga net indicates the importance of this
area to the Cahuilla. Although the specific location of these
sites is not indicated in the literature, we have tentatively
located Con kish wi qual (Site 274), and with more assurance,
Na hal log wen et, Snow Creek (Site 96), and Ta mare, Whitewater Point (Site 97).

Whitewater Canyon was the home territory of the Wanakik
lineage of the Wanakik sib, a favored wintering home of many
of the Wanakik people according to Bean's informant, Victoria
Wierick (Bean field notes, ca. 1960). The families living
there moved away sometime in the late 1800s after a flash flood
destroyed the main village site. They moved to Malki, sometimes referred to as Potrero, or Genio's Village. This is
now the Morongo Reservation. Descendants of the Wanakik
Wanakik lineage include the Pablo family at Morongo Reservation.

The Cahuilla name of the Whitewater Canyon village site
was Wanüp (Benedict 1924:112; Bean 1960:112). This is CSRI

Site 189. H. C. James (1960:38-39) maps a Cahuilla village in this area. Although it has been given the CSRI number 120, it is probable that he referred to Wanüp, and that CSRI Sites 120 and 189 are the same village. See Site 189, Chapter III.

The Whitewater Canyon area is an area of high sensitivity to contemporary Cahuilla Indians. From the point of view of ethnographers and archaeologists, the area has not been sufficiently studied and deserves serious study in cooperation with Native Americans. Some Native Americans at Morongo Reservation, however, have indicated that they are extremely reluctant to have further research done in the area at this time.

To the east of Whitewater Canyon is an area called Devil's Garden, Site 219. This is an area where many different kinds of cactus grow, and was traditionally an important food-gathering place for the Wanakik Cahuilla, and in recent years for many others. Barrel cacti are plentiful there. This species was a primary food resource for the Cahuilla, particularly in the spring months (See Bean and Saubel 1972:67-68).

Cottonwood Canyon, Site 334, was also an important food collecting and gathering site for Cahuilla Indians. Several archaeological sites have been reported in the area. Indigenous plant and animal food resources in this area are numerous, as they are throughout this part of the secondary study area. Several significant trails have been recorded crisscrossing this area (Johnston 1960).

Site 111, Kawishmu, was recorded by Kroeber as the name of "a small hill east of White Water, marking a boundary between the Wanupiapayum and the desert Cahuilla" (1908).

2-48

A view of the Santa Rosa Mountains showing the aridity of the environment and the steepness of the terrain. Photo taken 1978 by M. S. Crowley.

A view of Rockhouse Valley in the Santa Rosa Mountains. Doug Romoli provides scale in center of the photograph. Photo by Eric W. Ritter, 1978.

CHAPTER III. INDIVIDUAL SITES

Agua Alta Canyon (315)

This canyon, which lies between Toro Canyon and Pinyon Alta Flat, is in an area important for Cahuilla hunting and gathering.

Agua Alta Spring (14)

This spring is on the Cactus Spring Trail near Pinyon Alta Flat, and was an important source of water for those who used the trail.

Agua Bonita Spring (32)

This spring was along the main trail up Palm Canyon, where it would have been an important source of water for travellers, hunters, and those going up the canyon for ceremonial purposes.

Agua Fuerte Spring (323)

The name of this spring means "strong" water. It can be assumed to have supplied a substantial water supply for the upper West Fork of Palm Canyon.

Alder Canyon (325)

With Nicholias Canyon to the north, Alder Canyon formed the western part of Rockhouse Valley.

Andreas Canyon Trail (47)

This trail led up Andreas Canyon from its mouth up the south side of San Jacinto Mountain. It was used for hunting, gathering, and ritual travel.

Andreas Canyon Village (125)

See Andreas Canyon Discussion, pp. 2-35 to 2-38.

Archaeological Site of Clark Lake Dune Village (41)

This village site lies at the end of the trail from Rabbit Peak. It is about two acres in area, the largest in the region.

The oldest occupation is on an old dune surface at the north end of the site. This had been exposed by erosion. At the east end of the area on top of late dunes and on gravelly wash at the base of the Santa Rosa Mountains are the remains of a village presumably occupied at a later date. It is near mesquite and agave gathering places and was probably a winter dwelling place. Ben Squier, a relic collector, found a cremation associated with glass points and scrap iron here, and Malcolm Rogers found two cremations which had been washed out. One was associated with small-mouthed water ollas of "scoured" wear, two granite pestles, one granite mortar, two chalcedony points, and a granite mano. The other cremation was associated with a burnished pipe of "rid" wear and an incised, small-mouthed, buff-ware canteen three inches high (Anonymous, ca. 1938).

Asbestos Spring (28)

This spring lay at the northwestern corner of Pinyon Flat at the end of the trail from Palm Canyon. It was an important source of water for people harvesting pinyon nuts at Pinyon Flat. See Site 50, Pinyon Flat.

Ataki̅, Hidden Spring Village (45)

According to Juan Siva (Bean 1960a), this is the site of Ataki̅, the original home of the wantcinakiktum and palpunivi-kiktum clans of the Wildcat moiety (Strong 1929:41). The site is on a mesa above a hidden spring. It is possible that both early and late occupations are evidenced here. Some house pits were distinguishable in the 1930s. All had Caucasian material in them. One skull had a bandana handkerchief around the head (Anonymous, ca. 1938). See page 2-23 for further discussion.

Bear Creek (312)

A major trail ran along this creek from the La Quinta area to Little Pinyon Flat in the Santa Rosa Mountains.

Bear Creek Palm Oasis (215)

This is one of the many palm oases in the Cahuilla area (Henderson 1961:26). Even though there is no ethnographic data for the site, it can be assumed that it is a highly sensitive place to Native Americans because of the presence of a Washingtonia filifera eco-niche (Bean 1966; Bean and Saubel 1972:145-149).

Bear Creek Palms (17)

A palm oasis to which a trail led from both La Quinta and Palm Desert.

Big Falls (38)

This waterfall in Palm Canyon is famous to local desert travellers. Waterfalls have been important to the Cahuilla, often having been the locale of legendary events.

Bottle Gourd, Rockshelter (176)

A bottle gourd containing seeds was found in a rockshelter here (Bean and Saubel 1972).

Bradley Canyon (305)

This canyon goes from the desert to a series of trails which connected many villages, approximately along the route of Highway 111. The canyon was probably a hunting and gathering area. Patencio (1943), for example, mentions hunting and gathering in this general area. He mentions specifically Magnesia Spring Canyon and Cathedral Canyon. Bradley Canyon is near Trail 287, the Murray Hills trail.

Buck Ridge (326)

Buck Ridge forms the southern boundary of Rockhouse Valley. Its rugged character has kept the valley isolated.

Bullseye Rock (318)

This rock lies one mile from the main trail in Palm Canyon and seven miles south of Palm Springs.

Large rocks of this type are often sacred to the Cahuilla. They are often transformed nukatem from the Cahuilla time of creation, in illo tempore.

Ca wish is mal, Cathedral Canyon (91)

A place in Cathedral Canyon was named Ca wish is mal, "painted rock," by the Cahuilla culture hero, Evon ga net (Patencio 1943:53). It is an important site for Cahuilla culture history.

Cactus Spring Area (12)

The Cactus Spring area is one of the most sacred areas for the Cahuilla who lived in the desert, and one of the last ones untouched by modern developments. It contains the site of Weh-ghett, the "Place of the Ponderosa Pines," an important village, and a lower village named Tev-utt, "The Place of the Pinyon Trees." The area is mapped as Little Pinyon Flat. The sites of both Weh-ghett and Tev-utt contain many bedrock mortar grinding places, smooth rock floors where people used to dance, and many pictographs and petroglyphs. Four important trails go from here to the west, northeast, southeast, and southwest. Some of them are worn two feet deep in places.

The area still contains many plants and animals which were traditionally used by the Cahuilla, including a pinyon tree that is thought to be the "largest one anywhere." This is considered a sacred tree. The area is one of the few places where certain traditional medicine plants can still be found.

Cactus Spring Trail (13)

This important trail runs from Pinyon Flat near present-day Nightingale to Cactus Spring on Little Pinyon Flat in the Cactus Springs area (see Site 12), and continues to Pinyon Alta Flat on the southern slopes of Martinez Mountain, and thence to Martinez. Near Cactus Springs another trail branches off northeastward along Bear Creek down to La Quinta and still another goes westward toward Santa Rosa Mountain.

Katherine Saubel recalls that this was a trail by which her grandmother was taken as a young girl from the desert to the mountain home of her father's family when she was betrothed. It was also the trail used by people travelling to "Nukil" (funeral ceremonies) from some desert to some mountain villages.

Cahuilla Village, ca. 1895 (18)

This village, whose name was not recorded, was located in Palm Canyon about three miles south of Palm Springs in the extreme southwest corner of Section 35. The home of the chief was on the west side of the road to Rincon, and the other houses were situated across the road (Bennett 1948).

Carrizo Creek (310)

A major trail (Site 92) ran along this creek from the Palm Desert area to Pinyon Flat (Site 50).

Casa de Cuerva (317)

This large flat area in the Study Area lies above the village of Toro. It has been pointed out as the place where secret activities, such as boys' initiation rites, occurred in "the old days."

Cedar Spring (8)

A spring west of Virgin Spring on the same trail. At Cedar Spring the trail branches, one branch going northeastward to Cactus Spring.

Chaparrosa Spring (33)

This spring, on the eastern slopes of Chaparrosa Peak and at the head of Chaparrosa Wash would have been a source of water for Pass Cahuilla and Serrano people who lived within the secondary study area and hunted and gathered in the Sawtooth Range.

Clark Lake Petroglyph Trail (43T)

This trail leads from Site 42 to Site 46 to another site, location unknown, and eventually to Old Santa Rosa (Anonymous, ca. 1938).

Clark Lake Petroglyphs (42)

This petroglyph site lies at the base of the Santa Rosa Mountains, just east of the mouth of Rockhouse Canyon. The petroglyphs, which have been interpreted as being of an early Cahuilla type, are pecked into the reddish-brown patina of the boulders, which spread out for a hundred feet along trail 42T. There are agave fiber rubs associated with Site 42. These may be the same petroglyphs described and photographed by Reed (1963:116).

Clark Lake Rock Feature (40)

This feature near Clark Well, an important water source in the Colorado Desert, is near the southwest boundary of Rockhouse Canyon Cahuilla people's territory. Although it is about a mile outside the Study Area, it may be one of the most important Cahuilla sites in the Santa Rosa Mountains. It lay near the junction of trails, and there were pictographs and cobble shrines nearby. The feature consisted of boulders placed a foot and a half apart in a circle measuring 70 feet in diameter.

Con kish wi qual (274)

This place in Whitewater Wash was named Con kish wi qual by the Cahuilla culture hero, Evon ga net. The name means "two desert willows" (Patencio 1943:54). See discussion of the Whitewater area, pp. 2-46 to 2-48.

Conttonwood Canyon (334)

This area was occupied by Wanikik Cahuilla. There are many Cahuilla sites here, and Cahuillas of the area are sensitive to any possible encroachment or destruction by non-Indians.

Cottonwood Spring (5)

A spring in Rockhouse Valley.

In this century this is a site where water is close to the surface, but it is not a spring. It is half a mile from a village site, possibly that of Kēwel. After rains, the water here attracts "coyotes, bobcats, foxes, a few wild burros, desert birds, and an occasional Big Horn Sheep" (Reed 1963:122; Bean field notes, ca. 1960).

Cottonwood Springs Village Ruins (27)

These are probably the ruins of the village of Kēwel or Kīwil, occupied in the late 19th century by families of the sauicpakiktum lineage.   See discussion of the Santa Rosa and Rockhouse Canyon areas, pp. 2-14 to 2-27 and especially p. 2-21.

Cow on 'vah al ham ah, Indian Wells Point (85)

Not in Study Area.

Cox Ranch (337)

This ranch is in an area occupied by Cahuilla and then by Serrano, but does not appear specifically in the ethnographic literature.

Coyote Creek (15)

In the immediate precontact period, five lineages of the wiwaiistam clan lived in Coyote Canyon. One of these was the sauicpakiktum in the Thousand Palms Canyon off Collins Valley. It moved from there to Rockhouse Canyon and some of its members subsequently moved to the Torres-Martinez area. There has been a great deal of going back and forth from these places to Coyote Canyon, however (Strong 1929; Reed 1963; Merriam field notes; Bean field notes). See the discussion of the Santa Rosa and Rockhouse Canyon areas, pp. 2-14 to 2-27.

Dead Indian Creek Oasis (210)

This is a palm oasis along a creek which empties into Carrizo Creek (Henderson 1961:25). Our location is not exact.

Deep Canyon (128)

This canyon is important in the Cahuilla sacred literature as the home of Yellow Body (Patencio 1943:37), and as an occupied area. It was the site of a village at some time in the past, and has enormous floral and faunal potential.

Chase says it was called To-ho by the Indians, meaning "hunter-who-never-gets-his-game" (1919:30).

Devil Canyon (313)

This canyon runs from the edge of the desert into the Santa Rosa Mountains to the 6000 foot level. The canyon was easily accessible to Cahuilla living at Toro, La Quinta, and other places.

Devil's Garden (219)

The Devil's Garden is an area which contains a wider variety of cactus species than perhaps any other equivalent area of this size in the American Southwest. These species range from the miniature Mamillaria to the large Opuntias and Echinocactus, including the barrel cactus, which rivals the giant Sahuaro in size. Creosote bushes are interspersed among the cacti (James 1918:477).

Dos Palmas Spring (29)

Dos Palmas is a spring near the source of Carrizo Creek, which flows into the desert east of Cahuilla Hills and into the Palm Desert area. The spring is near the trail from Palm Desert to Pinyon Flat and there probably was a branch trail that led to it. It was probably the site of a palm oasis.

There was a place for training of young shamans at Dos Palmas (U.S. Department of the Interior, Bureau of Land Management, Ethnographic Notes 22, 1978). Because the site discussed there is a hot spring, we are inclined to believe that Dos Palmas on the east shore of the Salton Sea is the one referred to.

Ebbens Creek (308)

This creek joins with Dead Indian Creek (Sites 210 and 211), and Grapevine Creek (Site 212) to flow into Carrizo Creek (Site 310). These creeks provided a water supply for an important hunting area.

Eit (24)

Eit was the name given Murray Canyon by the "great net." The name means "thief" (Strong 1929:100; Bean field notes). See our discussion of Murray Canyon.

Fat mel mo (205)

A place in Palm Canyon. The name means "a place among many hills" (Patencio 1943:53).

"Fig Tree John" Petroglyphs (158)

Steward describes a group of petroglyphs at "Point Fig Tree John" near the road along the ancient shore of Lake Cahuilla. They are carved into travertine, apparently before the last rise of Lake Cahuilla, and were subsequently inundated. The travertine is composed of the shells of barnacle-like animals. The rock art is both carved and painted (1929: 84-85).

Fish Trap Petroglyphs (35)

These petroglyphs are close to the ancient Cahuilla fish traps (Site 34). Native Americans in the area consider them "national treasures," a symbol of their sacred past. They should be nominated for the National Register of Historic Places in order to be adequately protected and preserved.

Fish Traps (34)

Along what was the falling shoreline of ancient Lake Cahuilla lie a series of fish traps made of rocks, that were built by ancestors of the Cahuilla four or five hundred years ago. When the Colorado River changed its course, the huge freshwater lake began to dry up, a process that took fifty to sixty years, according to modern estimates. When the lake became too saline to support the growth of fish, these died by the thousands, and the Cahuilla built the fish traps to catch them as the waters receded. The experience lived on in their oral testimony. For example, Chase says, "When I spoke of the place to one of the Martinez Indians, he knew at once what I meant and referred to the objects unhesitatingly as 'the old fish traps'" (1919:176). Although many scholars ignored these oral traditions, recent work by Dr. P. Wilke now confirms their use as fish traps and demonstrate the significance of those in Cahuilla economic history.

The traps extend for some distance along the ancient shoreline. They are very important to the Cahuilla people as historical features (Wilke 1976:178-180; James 1918:240).

Forks Spring (338)

Although this spring is not specifically mentioned in the ethnographic literature, it is an important source of water in the highly significant Mission Creek area, important for both Cahuilla and Serrano occupation.

Gash mo (297)

This sandy spot, to the east of the "Garden of Eden" at the mouth of Palm Canyon, was named by Cahuilla culture hero Evon ga net. The name signified "the sounds of crunching sand as one walks" (Patencio 1943:53).

"Gordon Trail" (209)

This trail connected Andreas Canyon with the mouth of Palm Canyon (Jaeger 1953:13).

Grapevine Creek Palm Oasis (212)

This is a palm oasis on Grapevine Creek near the Shumway ranch.

Guadalupe Creek (314)

This creek runs down a canyon from the Santa Rosa Mountains, having its source on Martinez Mountain. It flows into the desert three or four miles northwest of Toro, coming out in the same place as Devil's Canyon.

Haviñavitcum territory (63)

The Haviñavitcum (Gifford 1918:191) or Havina Wanakik (Bean 1960:112), a lineage of the Wanakik Cahuilla, lived at Palm Springs Station in the early 19th century. Although they had their homes down on the desert and probably outside the Study Area, they would have used the secondary Study Area for hunting, gathering, and various ceremonial events.

Haystack Mountain (307)

This is a prominent mountain in the Study Area. Most such peaks were named, and it may still be possible to find out its Cahuilla name, although it does not, to our knowledge, appear in the ethnographic literature nor did the Cahuilla interviewed for this study recall the name.

Hermit's Bench Palm Oasis (156)

An oasis at the mouth of Palm Canyon (Henderson 1941: 26). See p. 2-35.

Hiawat (275)

Hiawat is a ridge in the Santa Rosa Mountains. According to Chase, Cahuilla leader Juan Razon ("Fig Tree John") showed him an aged document in which the great Cahuilla chief Cabezon had appointed Razon as capitan of Agua Dulce Tuba village, and owner of all the territory "running from the last low ridge of the Santa Rosas (the ridge was named Hiawat on the map, evidently an Indian word...) as far as Conejo Prieto or Black Rabbit Peak" (1919:182).

Hidden Gulch Palms (37)

This palm oasis lies on a trail at the foot of Murray Hill back of Palm Springs. The oasis is about a quarter of a mile outside the Study Area. It would have been used by people hunting and gathering in the Murray Hill area.

Hidden Palms Creek Palm Oasis (214)

This is an oasis, near the Palms to Pines Highway, and occupied in recent years by a non-Indian (Henderson 1961).

Hidden Spring (6)

A spring at Jackass Flat in Rockhouse Canyon, near which lies the site of the village of Ataki (Bean field notes 1960; Reed 1963:120).

Horse Portrero Canyon (306)

This is a tributary of Palm Canyon, and was a connecting link with the Los Coyotes area. It has a long history of occupation and use by the Cahuilla (Strong 1929; Reed 1963).

Indian Spring (322)

This spring provided an important source of water for the West Fork of Palm Canyon.

Indio Mountain (232)

This mountain, or hill, southwest of Indian Wells, was the southeastern boundary mark for the Kawisiktum lineage. It was called alhavik, meaning "an opening" (Strong 1929:101).

Isilsiveyaiutcem (78)

A village at Martinez Canyon to which the wantcinakiktum moved after puichekiva "broke up." See page 2-40.

Iviatim (2)

Iviatim was a Cahuilla village at the site of a warm spring near present-day Oasis. The vicinity was known as Agua Dulce earlier in this century. It was the home of the kaunukalkiktum ("living at kaunukvela") clan, who had seven houses there at one time, including the home of a religious and political leader or net (a ceremonial house), and of the iviatim lineage, who also had seven houses, but shared the net of the kaunukalkiktum. The iviatim were subordinate to the kaunukalkiktum at the earliest period remembered by Strong's informant Francisco Nombre, but may have been an older lineage rather than a branch of the clan.

The houses of the two groups were on either side of the spring, which was in the center of the village. Although the spring at iviatim is outside the Study Area, the area to the west of the spring, where the people from the village carried on hunting, gathering, and ceremonial activities, is within the Study Area (Strong 1929:39,42,50).

Jackass Flat (327)

Jackass Flat is the site of Hidden Spring (Ataki, Site 6). Rockhouse Canyon connects Jackass Flat and Rockhouse Valley. Jackass Flat was therefore an important occupation area.

Juan Razon's Allotment (163)

This forty acres in Section 28, Township 8 south, R. 9 east, was the allotment of Juan Razon, "Fig Tree John" (Beidler 1977). See discussion of Site 1.

Kahvinish, Indian Wells (Cov in ish, Kah-ve' nish) (69)

Merriam (field notes, date unknown) noted that the tribes who lived at Indian Wells ranged south into the desert mountains to Indio Mountain and Sheep Mountain and west to Deep Canyon.

Kauissimtcem hempkĭ (233)

This hill, four miles south of Palm Springs, was named by the "great net" (Strong 1929:101).

Kaukwicheki (227)

The "great net" gave the name kauwicheki to a "stream where hunters and acorn gatherers camped" (Strong 1929:100). Its exact location is unknown.

Kaunukvela (52)

The site of kaunukvela, original home of the kaunukal-kiktum clan who lived at iviatim (Site 2) during the late nineteenth century, is near Bautiste (Strong 1929:42,50).

Kawishmu (111)

Kroeber (1908:35) gives Kawishmu as the name of "a small hill east of Whitewater, marking the boundary between the Wanupiapayum and the desert Cahuilla."

Kwa le ki (70)

This is the site of a small village at Pinyon Flats described by Barrows (1900:27): "These villages seem to have been halfway camps between the desert and the mountain rancherias farther on, and probably never more than a few families occupied them at a time. The elevation is five or six thousand feet higher than the desert, and the air is bracing and fine."

Although Alice Lopez is not familiar with the name Kwa le ki, she says there was a camping place at Pinyon Flat where they used to stop when they went to Santa Barbara (Vane field notes, 1979).

La Quinta (218)

This is a well-known area of Cahuilla settlement. A major trail complex leads from it into the Santa Rosa Mountains.

Lake Cahuilla Shoreline (206)

The ancient shoreline of Lake Cahuilla which can be seen up from the present shoreline of the Salton Sea that now fills some of the same basin, was an aboriginal hunting and gathering area (Romero 1954; Wilke 1976:22).

Little Clark Lake (58)

There were areas in this dry lake where water was close enough to the surface to support large areas of mesquite growth. Hence this was a mesquite gathering place for the Cahuilla, who would come to the mesquite groves each season. Antelope and various small game animals and birds were hunted in the area (Bean field notes, ca. 1960).

Mad Woman Spring (319)

This spring is a source of water, now part of the Agua Caliente Reservation.

Magnesia Spring (31)

This spring is the source of water in Magnesia Spring Canyon, which Patencio (1943:71) says was included in the Murray Hills trail system.

Magnesia Spring Canyon (90)

The main Murray Hill trail mentioned by Patencio (1943) crosses at the mouth of this canyon, which was called

Pah-wah-te, "the drinker," by the Cahuilla. See Site 287.

Maringa (197)

This was one of the homes of the Maringa clan of the Serrano. It was located where Big Morongo Creek opened into Morongo Valley, according to Benedict (1924:368).

Martinez Canyon (288)

See Martinez Canyon discussion, pp. 2-40 to 2-42.

Martinez Mountain (303)

This mountain was a major area for Cahuilla hunting, gathering, and sacred activity.

Mauūlmiī (23)

The site of the principal village at Toro, said to have been the home of the tamolanitcem; and of the sawalakiktum, who before that lived at La Mesa with the Nanhaīyum. This information is from Gifford (1918:189-191), who received it from three informants. He notes that none of the clan names they gave him corresponded with the "names of present-day Cahuilla villages listed by Dr. D. P. Barrows" (1900). The sawalakiktum, therefore, were apparently the occupants of the site in the late prehistoric period.

According to Strong, the wakaīkiktum ("night heron"), panakauissiktum ("water fox"), and, later, the sewahilem lineages lived at Mauūlmiī in the late 1870s (Strong 1929: 52). See discussion of Toro Canyon, pages 2-43 to 2-44.

Milyillikalet (93)

The "great net" gave this name to a place at the mouth of Andreas Canyon (Strong 1929:101). Twelve bedrock mortars, two arrow straighteners, two bone awls and potsherds were found here by archaeologist Herb Samson in 1938. See pp. 2-37 to 2-38.

Mission Creek home of Kilyiñakiktum clan (61)

Gifford (1918:190) says that the Cahuilla Kilyiñakiktum lineage lived at Mission Creek, presumably before the Serrano came into the area. Bean's informants said a Wainikik lineage lived there (Bean field notes, 1959).

3-14

Mission Creek Trail (340)

This was an important trail for the Cahuilla and Serrano who lived in the Mission Creek area, leading up the San Bernardino Mountains.

Mountain Home Spring (11)

A spring on Virgin Spring trail west of Santa Rosa Spring.

Mukunpat (191)

Gifford says Mukunpat was the name of a clan of the Wildcat Moiety that lived with the Morongo and Mohiyanim clans, originally in Bear Valley, but also at Yamisevul (Site 190) in the Mission Creek area, Maringa (Site 197), and Türka (Site 198) (1918:180). Benedict says that Mukunpat was a place name for the Mühiatnim territory (1924:368). The location of the site is approximate.

Murray Hills Trail (287)

This trail went from the "Garden of Eden" back of Palm Springs past Eagle Spring, Magnesia Canyon, Cathedral Canyon, and on into the Deep Canyon area to join other trails (Patencio 1943:71).

Na hal log wen et, Snow Creek (96)

The Cahuilla culture hero Evon ga net crossed from Whitewater Point to Snow Creek, which he called Na hal log wen et, meaning "the center of an open place" (Patencio 1943:54).

Nicholias Canyon, Spring, and Village (203)

Nicholias Canyon opens into Rockhouse Valley. See page 2-25.

Old Santa Rosa Ruins (16)

See Santa Rosa area/Rockhouse Canyon discussion, Chapter II.

Olla Cache (44)

An ambiguous statement on site record C-134 (Site 42)
suggests that a site for which the records is missing, Site
C-146, contained a few sherds and a cache of ollas, which
were collected by a Mr. Wear of Imperial Valley. The sherds
and ollas may have been found at Site 42, 46, or at Old
Santa Rosa (See Santa Rosa area/Rockhouse Canyon) (Anonymous
ca. 1938). The location of Site 44 is between Site 46 and
Old Santa Rosa.

"One Palm Creek" (213)

This spring with one palm is near the mouth of Deep
Canyon. Even though there is but the one palm, this is
likely to have been a spot where hunters and travellers
camped (Henderson 1961).

Painted Sign Marks in Andreas Canyon (51)

Patencio says that there used to be painted signs, pictographs, all over the country, marking trails and conveying
other important information. Only some of them are still
understood. They have been replaced by printed signs and road
markers. "People no longer depended on them for the way and
water. There are the painted sign marks in Andreas Canyon,
but no one reads them today, they are fast fading now"
(Patencio 1943:103).

Palhīliwit ("Wide Water") (19)

Palhīliwit was a village about two miles south of where
the Martinez Reservation buildings are now. It had a spring
which provided sufficient water for some irrigation and for
swimming in hot weather. It was the home of three clans:
the mumletcem, who owned the spring and are remembered as
having eight houses; the masuwitcem, who had seven houses;
and the wiitem, who had five houses. Each clan had its own
net and dance house. All belonged to the Coyote moiety.
The area to the west in the primary Study Area would have
been used by these clans for hunting, gathering, and ceremonial activities.

Palm Canyon Trail (207T)

This important trail led south from the Palm Springs
area through Palm Canyon to the Mesquite Flat area, and on
to Vandeventer Flat and the Santa Rosa/Rockhouse Canyon area.

Palm Canyon Trail Shrines (157)

Piles of pebbles or small rocks beside the trail up Palm Canyon. See p. 2-34 (Henderson 1941).

Palms to Pines Trail (92)

This trail from the Palm Desert area up Carrizo Creek Canyon to Pinyon Crest on the edge of Pinyon Flat and then east to Deep Canyon, was an extremely important trail. It was used by desert peoples going into the mountains for pinyon harvesting, other gathering, hunting, and ceremonial events. The modern Palms to Pines highway follows it for some way from Palm Desert, but is less direct in the mountain area.

Palo Verde Canyon (331)

An ancient trail runs down this canyon to the natural rock tanks in Smoke Tree Canyon. This area was frequented by mountain sheep (Reed 1963).

Palo Verde Spring (56)

This spring was an important water supply at the head of Palo Verde Canyon in the Santa Rosa Mountains. This was an area where mountain sheep were hunted (Reed 1963:116-117).

Palpūniviktum hemkī (291)

Palpūniviktum hemkī was a village two miles east of Alamo (which was south of 74th Avenue on Peirce Street). It was the home of the palpunivikiktum clan, and two lineages apparently subordinate to that clan: the tēviñakiktum and the tamulañitcum. These groups were respectively from atakī, tevi and palīliem hemkī in the Santa Rosa Mountains. Each group in general had different gathering areas in the mountains, but they shared an area due west of Alamo, called ēova, for gathering cactus in the spring and summer. Barrows recorded the names Lawilvan ("cottonwood") and Sivel ("sycamore") for this village, according to Strong, but Barrows says that these names were given the site of Alamo (1900:34). Strong's informants did not recognize these names. Strong also says that Palsīkal, "water hole," was an old name for Palpūniviktum hemkī (1929:41,50).

Paltūkwic kaīkaīawit (1)

    This location had a warm spring and sufficient water
for domestic uses, but not for irrigation. It lay beside
the Salton Sea, and the wantciñakik ramianawitcem clan
moved there from Tūva, two miles south, about 1880. This
was the clan of Juan Razon, generally known as "Fig Tree
John." Gifford (1918) had reported Fig Tree John's clan
as the Palkausinakela. Strong says "this was given as the
place name of the site where Fig Tree John lived later"
(1929:49). It is not clear from Strong's text whether
Palkausinakela also referred to Paltūkwic kaīkaīawit.

    According to Alice Lopez, Juan Razon began to raise
figs after some white people gave him some plants. (Team-
sters on the Bradshaw trail used to stop at his place to
change horses, and buy bundles of hay.) Alice remembers
that Juan's son Jack Razon and his wife brought figs to
her family when she was young. At first the children were
reluctant to eat something so strange.

    Juan had two sons, Jack and Mike Razon.

    Alice's family used to go to Juan Razon's to visit,
and she remembers him telling stories about the water
babies that cried in his spring, especially if someone
were going to die. Once in a while they could be seen on
top of the water. They had red skin, and no hair. When
they saw someone coming, they rolled back into the water.
Water babies were also heard at the hot springs at Palm
Springs (Vane 1970, 1979).

Palukiki, Stubbe Canyon (188)

    This canyon was part of the territory owned by the
Wanakik Cahuilla sib. Many archaeological sites have
been recorded within it. Benedict reports it as the home
of the Palukiktam group, which she mistakenly thought to be
Serrano, and gave the place name as Palukiki (1924:368).
Strong gave it the place name Paluknavitcem (1929:91).
Bean's informant, Victoria Wierick, identified the group
that lived there as the Palukna Wanakik lineages of the
Wanakik sib, one of ten languages of the sib that were
active in the early 19th century. It is no longer cere-
monially active.

Pa-nach-sa (193)

This is a mountain camp or village on the north side of Toro Peak described by Barrows as "high up on the north side of Torres" (1900:27). Its exact location is unknown.

Panyik (26)

According to Strong, the "great net" very long ago brought his people first to watcicpa (Redland junction), then to īva, a hot spring north of Soboba, to kekliva, a mountain north of Soboba, and then to panyik at the mouth of San Andreas Canyon (1929:100). This place name is associated with the Paniktum lineage, which has been and is associated with the lower San Andreas and Palm Canyons. See our discussion of Palm Springs area, pp. 2-27 to 2-35.

Pa:tsh yara:'nka' Wanet (217)

Pa:tsh yara:'nka' Wanet, according to Hill (1973:217), was the Serrano name for the Whitewater River, a stream important as a source of water and for the flora and fauna which it supported. See discussion of the Whitewater area.

Paskwa (221)

This hot spring is halfway up Palm Canyon. Nearby are rock mortars (Strong 1929:100). It was named by the "great net." See discussion of Palm Canyon.

Petroglyphs in Rockhouse Canyon (46)

This is a petroglyph site on the Clark Sink Trail (Anonymous, ca. 1938).

Pictograph Site (216)

A pictograph site in Andreas Canyon (Smith and Turner 1975).

Pierce Ranch and Springs (346)

This area figured in Willie Boy's flight (Lawton 1960). Willie Boy has the character now of a legendary figure among Cahuillas and Chemehuevis.

Pīnalata, Kalahal (225)

The "great net" named these two places northwest of
sīmuta (Strong 1929:100). Their exact location is unknown.
They are probably not in the Study Area. Pīnalata is a flat.

Pinyon Flat (50)

Pinyon Flat was a uniquely valuable place for food collecting and hunting game for the Cahuilla. The area was used
by many groups, but apparently not owned by any particular
group. Informants in the 1960s recalled to Bean that pinyon
crops were available to whomever was able to get there first.
People from many villages from Cahuilla Valley and from the
villages that lay at the mouths of Palm Canyon, San Andreas
Canyon, Deep Canyon, Martinez Canyon, and Santa Rosa Canyon--
all would come into the area when the pinyon nuts were ready
for harvesting and camp there for a short time, and then leave.

Alice Lopez remembers that her mother used to tell of
going along to harvest pinyon at Pinyon Flat when she was
young, which would have been in the 1860s or 1870s. She rode
horseback from Martinez, where she lived, up Martinez Canyon,
accompanying her uncle. Before they picked any nuts they
put food in the Big House for three days, and sang ceremoni-
ally--a first fruits rite. Alice's mother's task was to
carry water for the nut pickers. Picking nuts was hard
work. Someone had to climb the trees and hit the pine cones
with sticks to get them loose. They were put in sacks (they
made the hands sticky) and carried home. Then a fire of
brush was built in the sand, and the nuts were buried over-
night in the hot sand pit. In the morning they were taken
out and pounded on a rock to make the seeds come out. They
stayed at the Flat for a week.

At Santa Rosa, Alice's mother's sister put food in the
Big House for three days before going to Pinyon Flat (Vane
field notes, 1979).

Pinyon Flat lay at a place where the boundaries of many
clans' territories met. Its function as a "common area" had
the effect of limiting conflict over a valuable food resource
which was unstable. In contrast to acorn producing oaks and
mesquite trees, the pinyons were erratic in their production
from year to year while the former were stable. Given the
stability of the acorn and mesquite bean supplies, the political energy necessary to maintain strict ownership rules with
respect to pinyons was probably non-efficient for the Cahuilla.
The enforcement of the rules would have led to conflict (Bean
1972:129; Bean and Saubel 1972:102-105).

Potrero Spring (30)

This spring lies on the trail between Palm Canyon and Pinyon Flat, and was an important source of water for people travelling from Palm Canyon to Pinyon Flat where they went to gather pinyon nuts each year and for other reasons such as hunting and gathering other food resources.

Possible Site of Early Agricultural Beginnings (186)

"The late Juan Siva, born in 1872, stated that his grandfather planted crops at the southern edge of Rabbit Peak near Martinez and at Thousand Palms in Borrego Valley" (Bean and Saubel 1972:206).

Puichekiva (22)

A village site within what is now Torres-Martinez Reservation. The name meant "Road Runner's House." This was one of the most important Cahuilla villages in the desert from perhaps about 1850. It was the home of Strong's consultant, Francisco Nombres, and was used by Strong as an example of a "typical Desert Cahuilla village of fifty-odd years ago." The village broke up because of a water shortage when the water table fell about the turn of the century (Strong 1929:45-49; Bean field notes).

Pulukla (228)

The "great net" called "a hill to which hunters would sing in the dance house in order to have deer sent them" pulukla (Strong 1929:100). It is probably the peak that is called Spitler's Peak today.

Rattlesnake Canyon (329)

This area was an important area for hunting, especially for mountain sheep, which frequented the rock tanks and springs in the area for water (Reed 1963).

Rattlesnake Spring (4)

A permanent spring in Santa Rosa Mountains. It was an important water source for hunters. Near it is the site of an Indian camp or village (Reed 1963:126).

Rattlesnake Spring (4)

A permanent spring in Santa Rosa Mountains. It was an important water source for hunters. Near it is the site of an Indian camp or village (Reed 1963:120).

Rock Tanks (57)

These rock tanks lie near the head of Smoke Tree Canyon and at the end of a trail coming up Palo Verde Wash. They are likely to have been an important source of water to travellers and hunters in this part of the Anza-Borrego Desert.

Rock Tanks (352)

These are natural rock tanks at about 2000 feet elevation in the Santa Rosa Mountains. Reed reports seeing five of them, and another up the mountain to the east. He says the old-timers called them sheep tanks because "of the Big Horn Sheep watering there after heavy rains when these holes in the boulders are filled with water as the water runs down the canyons that have such places in the bottoms" (1963:117). It must be assumed that these were important to Native American hunters not only for the water they held, but also for the wild life they attracted, especially the sheep. There is a picture of one of the tanks in Reed (1963:119).

Rockhouse Valley Peppergrass Gathering Area (173)

An area in Rockhouse Valley where peppergrass was gathered (Bean and Saubel 1972).

San Gorgonio Pass (110)

This pass, part of which lies within a mile of the secondary Study Area, is and has always been exremely important as the lowest pass between the Colorado desert areas through the intervening mountains to the Los Angeles Basin. Indian trails converged here just as roads, railroad tracks, and transmission lines do today.

San we yet, Vandeventer Flat (89)

This site figures in Cahuilla oral literature (Patencio 1943:37-38). It has had early and late occupations, being presently on the Santa Rosa Reservation. It was once part of the Vandeventer Ranch. See pages 2-24 to 2-25.

(New) Santa Rosa, Sēwia, or Sēwĭu, or We-wut-now-hu (60)

A village on the south slope of Santa Rosa mountain on
what later was the Vandeventer Ranch and is now part of Santa
Rosa Reservation. One lineage of the sauicpakiktum lineage
moved there from Thousand Palms Canyon off Collins Valley in
the late 19th century (Barrows 1900:37; Kroeber 1925:694;
James 1918; Strong 1929:145-146). See pages 2-16 to 2-17, 2-24.

Santa Rosa Spring (10)

A spring on Virgin Spring trail west of Stump Spring.

Sewĭ (223)

Sewĭ is noted as marking the southwestern boundary of
the territory of the Kawisiktum clan. It was named by the
"great net" and lies at the south end of Palm Canyon (Strong
1929:100). It was probably near to or the same as Se'-o-ye
(Smith 1909) at Vandeventer Flat or Sēwia (Strong 1929:145-
157). See discussion, pp. 2-14 to 2-27.

Sēwitckul (25)

This is the name given Murray Hill by the "great net"
(Strong 1929:100). See our discussion of Murray Hill area.

Sheep Canyon (328)

This canyon in the Santa Rosa Mountains west of the
Salton Sea was a hunting and gathering area for the people
who lived in Agua Dulce and Iviatim. This whole area was
frequented by mountain sheep.

Sherman Shady Spring (345)

This spring was a water source for the Maringa clan of
Serranos who lived at Sites 191 and 197.

Sim mo ta, or Tev koo hul ya me (295)

The Cahuilla culture hero, Evon ga net "came down near
to what is now called Palm Canyon. He called this country
Sim mo ta, meaning Indian corral or pasture" (Patencio 1943:
53).

Sīmūta (224)

The "great net" named a place with "more rock mortar holes, about five miles west of Palm Canyon" sīmūta (Strong 1929:100). The exact location of this is not known.

Smoke Tree Canyon (332)

A canyon in the eastern Santa Rosa Mountains. It is marked by the presence of natural rock tanks which provided a source of water for mountain sheep and wild life as well as Indians while in the area. The sides of the canyons show many trails, apparently made by sheep (Reed 1963).

Springs (301)

This spring off Deep Canyon, not specifically mentioned in the ethnographic literature, was an important source of water in a canyon which led from the north slope of Santa Rosa Mountain to Pinyon Flat.

Still's Landing and Millard Canyon Trail (344)

This area was occupied by Cahuilla and Serrano peoples.

Stump Spring (9)

A spring on a small trail that branches off the Virgin Spring trail west of Cedar Spring. This small trail goes north and west, ending at Stump Spring.

Ta co wits, Taquitz Mountain (86)

See discussion of Taquitz concept.

Tatmīlmī (222)

Tatmīlmī, at the south end of Palm Canyon, where it enters Vandeventer Flat, was given its name by the Cahuilla culture hero, the "great net" (Strong 1929:100).

Taupakic (230)

The "great net" named a place southeast of Murray Hill taupakic, which means "mescal gathering place." It probably was a place in Cathedral Canyon (Strong 1929:101).

Tcial (226)

The "great net" named a hill northwest of Palm Canyon tcial, meaning "head with feathers in the hair" (Strong 1929: 100). Its exact location is unknown.

Tcīuk (293)

The wakaīkiktum clan from Toro were originally from "tcīuk in the Santa Rosa Mountains" (Strong 1929:41).

Tekic (94)

Pictograph found at the entrance to Andreas Canyon. See pp. 2-35 to 2-36.

Temelmekmekuka (21)

Temelmekmekuka (Strong 1929:41), also spelled "temelmek- meka," was two miles from puīchekiva (Site 22), where the Narbonne-Martinez ranch was in 1929. The wantcauem clan had lived at temelmekmekuka before they moved to puīchekiva, having had part of its homes destroyed by a flash flood which came down Martinez Canyon (Strong 1929:41,68). Martinez Canyon in the Study Area would have been part of the territory in which the clan had hunting and gathering rights.

Temelsēkalet (20)

Temelsēkalet was a village half a mile south of where the Martinez Reservation buildings are now. It was the home of the autaatem clan, some of whose members still lived there in the 1920s. Six houses were clustered around a well, which provided enough water for some agriculture. There were also some communally owned mesquite trees nearby.

The autaatem clan went to the mountains together with the awilem clan from Puīchekiva in the spring, and shared nearby food areas with the other clan. These areas were in part within the Study Area, in the Martinez Canyon area. The two clans may have started out as lineages of an older clan.

Temukvall (234)

The "great net" named this "low hill on edge of desert near here, where a man watched when they hunted rabbits" (Strong 1929:101). The rabbit hunters that the man watched were the nukatem, people of the Cahuilla creation time, in illo tempore.

Tev ing el we wy wen it (49)

A place near Palm Canyon whose name meant "a round flat
basket closed up at the top, that is hung up." The son of
Ca wis ke on ca moved here and raised a large family (Patencio 1943:90). See page 2-30.

Tevin' imulwi-waiwinut (220)

This is a flat rock with mortar holes in it. It is
at the mouth of Palm Canyon. See discussion of Palm Canyon.
(Strong 1929:100).

Toro (64)

An important settlement area for the Cahuilla from
prehistoric times; now a part of Torres-Martinez Reservation.
See discussion, pages 2-43 to 2-46.

Toro Cemetery (36)

This cemetery is associated with Toro (Torres Reservation). Members of the waikaikiktum (Strong 1929:52), pronounced
"waikwoikiktum" by Alice Lopez (Vane 1979), are
buried generally in the western part of the cemetery; members
of the Levi family in the center, and of the Duros from Santa
Rosa in the eastern part of it, according to Alice Lopez
(Vane 1979). See discussion of Toro Canyon area, pp.
2-43 to 2-46, and especially 2-46.

Toro Wells (39)

The Cahuilla built walk-in wells to provide themselves
with a water supply before contact with Europeans. They
continued to dig such wells after contact. In the late 19th
century there were eight wells at Toro, at that time used for
irrigation of mesquite and other food plants. Some of the
wells survived at least into the 1930s (Barrows 1900:26-27;
Baldwin 1938). See page 2-45.

Trail and Associated Features (351T)

This trail leads from Palo Verde Wash to the Natural
Rock Tanks in the Santa Rosa Mountains, thence to Wonderstone
Wash and the Salton Sea. The rock tanks apparently were a
great attraction for mountain sheep, and there are many sheep
trails leading to them. Going further on this trail, Reed
found another small tank near the trail. There were mescal

pits, and other signs of an Indian camp site beside the tank. Across the main ridge of the mountains he found indications of two other camp sites showing signs of Indian habitation. He also found two rock cairns and several metates along the trail, and believes it was once "one of the main travel ways to the Salton Sea area" (Reed 1963:116-118). This trail would have to be walked to establish its exact location.

Trail between Nicolas Canyon and Santa Rosa Reservation (354T)

Reed says, "Of the old Indian trails leading to and from Rockhouse Valley is one between the present Santa Rosa Reservation and Nicolas Canyon that is still used by persons going to or from Rockhouse on foot or on horseback" (1963:126). The location of this trail can only be estimated.

Trail from Clark Dry Lake to Rabbit Peak (278T)

This trail goes up steeply from the site of Clark Lake Dune village to an elevation of 5000 feet in the course of four miles, ending on Rabbit Peak. There are numerous olla sherds on the way. See discussion of Clark Lake Dune village, Site 41.

Trail from Coyote Canyon to Hidden Spring (349T)

"A trail leading from near the mouth of Coyote Canyon to Hidden Spring can still be followed; starting up North Canyon (Box Canyon) for about a mile, then up small side canyon for about the same distance to where the trail turns sharply to the right across several rocky ridges, then into some little valley-like places where the water stands for quite some time after heavy rainfall. Here again is evidence of the Indians having taken advantage of times when water was available for their camps while gathering food" (Reed 1963:113-114).

Trail from Horse Canyon to Hidden Spring (347T)

Reed described a trail that led from Coyote Canyon to the Santa Rosa Reservation. "A branch from this trail leading from the water in Horse Canyon across the mountain in a south-easterly direction to Hidden Spring, Clark Lake, and into the Rockhouse Valley areas. Along this branch of the trail are evidences of many of the mescal pits" (Reed 1963: 111-112).

It would be necessary to walk this trail to locate it precisely.

Trail from Middle Willows to Hidden Spring (348T)

Reed describes a trail from Middle Willows, "across the rugged mountain to the east is another one of the Indians' travel-ways leading to Hidden Spring.... Along this trail after one travels across the rough mountains, there is considerable evidence of the Indians having lived there, at least when gathering food. Near the larger granite boulders can be found small pieces of broken pottery and signs of the mescal pits" (1963:113).

It would be necessary to walk this trail to locate it precisely.

Trail from Rockhouse Valley to Toro Peak (355T)

"The old trail leading from Rockhouse Valley to the north on Toro Peak is said to be extremely difficult any more because of its not being used and due to heavy rains that have fallen through the years" (Reed 1963:126). Reed does not give any more information about the location of this trail.

Trail in Rockhouse Valley (165T)

This trail went from village Site 27 to Site 16 in Rockhouse Valley. These are very old village sites. See pp. 2-14 to 2-27.

Trail to Clark Lake and Hidden Spring (350T)

"An Indian trail that is still easy to follow whenever it was not in the sand washes, leads into the Clark Lake area, with a branch leading to Hidden Spring. This trail comes across a rough ridge extending to the north from Butler Mountain, and was used by the Clark brothers when taking supplies to their cow-camp. This trail starts across this rough ridge directly across the valley from the Doc Beaty Place (Anza Ranch)" (Reed 1963:116).

Travertine Palms Wash (3)

This wash must be assumed from its name to have held a palm oasis. It would have been an important part of the territory of the people who lived at paltukwic kaĩkaĩawit (CSRI Site 67) (Strong 1929:49).

Travertine Rocks Cave and Petroglyphs (159)

The travertine rocks are the remains of an ancient

island, covered with a thick layer of calcium carbonate, the
remains of the shells of marine animals. Chase found a cave
on the northeast side of this outcrop, about 60 feet deep,
and containing pottery sherds, but no traces of smoke on the
ceiling and minimal plant life. He interpreted these details
to mean the cave was a place of refuge (1919:186).

Steward described petroglyphs on the rocks. They are
carved in the travertine, and dated from various periods.
Some appeared to have been carved before the last rise of
Lake Cahuilla. One bore the date "1898" carved on the travertine. Plain pottery sherds were found at the western
base of the rocks (1929:87).

Türka (198)

Türka was one of the places owned by the Maringa clan
of Serranos. It was in "Morongo Valley, along the present
road" (Benedict 1924:368). Its exact location is unknown.

Tuva (54)

This village on the shores of the Salton Sea was the
home of the telakiktum clan originally, before the historic
period. Its members were all dead "when informants first
remembered the place." In the late 19th century it was the
home of the wantciñakik tamianawitcem clan, the clan of Juan
Razon, better known as Fig Tree John. The spring at Tuva
had water enough for domestic purposes, but not enough for
irrigation. This spring was known as Fish Springs. Tuva
is presently inundated by the Salton Sea.

Near Tuva in the late prehistoric period was another
village, ulicpatciat, where a clan named mumkwitcem (always
sick) had their home. All members of this clan had died
before Strong's informant, Francisco Nombres, was born
(Strong 1929:42, 49-50).

Üakī (298)

Original home of wīitem (grasshoppers) clan in Santa
Rosa Mountains (Strong 1929:42).

Upper Dead Indian Creek Trail (211)

This trail led into Deep Canyon, and led along the
creek, where there was a palm oasis (Henderson 1961:25).

Village Cremation Site (164)

A cremation site at the village site near Cottonwood
Springs, Site 27 (Minor 1976). See Santa Rosa/Rockhouse
Canyon discussion, pp. 2-14 to 2-27.

Village Site (59)

Village Site (200)

Site where isilsiva group moved from Ataki, according
to Juan Siva (Bean field notes, 1960).

Virgin Spring, Trail (7)

This spring is to the west of Toro Peak. It lies on
an important trail which leads westward down the mountain
and then north to Palm Canyon.

Wa wash ca le it (95)

The Cahuilla culture hero Evon ga net named the Murray
Hills Wa wash ca le it, "which means stripes on the hills...
and the same stripes or streaks are there today" (Patencio
1943:53).

Wanüp (189)

Wanüp, according to Benedict (1924:112) was the home of
the Wanapüpayam group of Serrano, a group subsequently
identified as the Wanakik Wanakik lineage of the Wanakik
sib of Cahuilla (Bean 1960b:112). Benedict places Wanüp at
the mouth of Whitewater Canyon. According to Bean's informant, Victoria Wierick, the Wanakik Wanakik also occupied
the area of the later Mission Creek Indian Reservation.
They moved to Malki from the Whitewater Canyon after a flood
destroyed their home prior to 1870. The exact location of
their village is not known.

The Wanakik Wanakik were one of ten lineages of the
Wanakik sib in the early part of the 19th century. Leader-
ship of the sib appears to have rested with the Wanakik
Wanakik lineage, which is the one which survives to this day
(Bean 1960b).

Watering Place for Wildlife (353)

Reed says that in summer, 1962, a "descendant of the Rockhouse Valley Indians (Art Guanche) and a fellow by the name of Henry 'Hank' Lichtwald developed the spring" at the village ruins at the base of Toro Peak (Site 16, probably Old Santa Rosa) "as a watering place for the wildlife of the area. The development of this watering place was a part of the game management program of the California Department of Fish and Game" (Reed 1963:123).

Weal um mo Mountain, Santa Rosa Mountain (84)

This mountain is a sacred mountain which figures prominently in Cahuilla oral literature. See page 2-26.

Well No. 1 (285)

This well was dug by the government in 1938.

West Fork, Palm Canyon Hunting Trail (48)

This hunting trail led up the west fork of Palm Canyon. Agua Fuerte Spring was the source of water in the canyon. The trail also led past another spring east of the canyon, Agua Caliente, Indian Spring. Also see Palm Canyon discussion, pp. 2-29 to 2-35.

Wilamū

Wilamū, in the Santa Rosa Mountains near Martinez Mountain, was the original home of the awilem clan, before they moved to awilsilhiwinina. Here they lived with the avtaatem clan who were relatives of theirs. The two clans gathered food and owned the territory jointly, according to Strong (1929:41,44).

Yamisevul, Mission Creek Area (190)

The Mission Creek territory was claimed by the Morongo clan, of the Coyote moiety of Serranos, as one of its original territories. The Cahuilla name for this clan, with whom they intermarried, was Marongam (Gifford 1918:179). This aboriginal territory should not be confused with Mission Creek Indian Reservation of the historical period. Benedict reports that the Serrano name for the site of the Marongam village was Yamisevul, meaning "where the yucca blossoms," and says that it was at the canyon mouth of Mission Creek. The clan also owned the territory at Site 197, Maringa, and Site 198, Türka (in Morongo Valley along the road in 1924) (Benedict 1924:368). The nature of aboriginal occupancy in this entire area is not well remembered by contemporary Serranos.

You koo hul ya me (294)

A place in Palm Canyon where Palm Canyon people are said to have dashed the skulls of their enemies. See p. 2-30.

GATHERING AREAS

Acorn Gathering Area, Upper Murray Canyon (184)

Upper Murray Canyon was an important acorn gathering site (Bean and Saubel 1972).

Agave Gathering Area, Deep Canyon (169)

"The sites of numerous agave roasting pits may be found also in the hills directly south of Palm Desert in the Deep Canyon region" (Bean and Saubel 1972:32).

Agave Gathering Area, Rabbit Peak (170)

Rabbit Peak is one of the specific agave-gathering areas which Cahuilla informants remembered (Bean and Saubel 1972:32).

Agave Gathering Area, Whitewater Canyon (168)

"The Wanikik Cahuilla of San Gorgonio Pass gathered agave near Whitewater Canyon" (Bean and Saubel 1972:32). They also gathered other plants in this canyon.

Barrel Cactus Gathering Area, Santa Rosa Mountains (174)

The buds and the mature flower of the barrel cactus were prized as food by the Cahuilla, the buds tasting something like artichokes when steamed. The body of the plant could be used as a cooking vessel. According to Cahuilla information, the cactus also served as a reservoir of water on the desert. Many of them were found on the southern slopes of the Santa Rosa Mountains (Bean and Saubel 1972:67).

Barrel Cactus Gathering Area, Whitewater Canyon (175)

An important source of barrel cacti for Cahuilla and Serrano in the Malki-Mission Creek area (Bean and Saubel 1972).

Greens Gathering Area, Vandeventer Flat (279)

The Cahuilla gathered greens in this area near Vandeventer Flat.

Manzanita Gathering Area (172)

Manzanitas, Arctostaphylos adans (kelel in Cahuilla) are common in the lower canyons of the San Jacinto Mountains near places where Cahuilla villages were located. Their fruits were used in beverage, to make an aspic-like substance, and dried to eat later. Manzanita wood was used for fires, and branches were used for house construction and to make tools. The berries also served to attract game (Bean and Saubel 1972:40-41). This is a site which has been specifically located as such an area.

Mesquite Gathering Area, Rockhouse Canyon (183)

Nearly every part of the mesquite, Prosopis juliflora, was used by the Cahuilla. The beans and blossoms were important food staples, second only to acorns as a major food resource. The stand at the mouth of Rockhouse Canyon was one of the most abundant in the Borrego Desert (Bean and Saubel 1972:107-108).

Opuntia Gathering Area (282)

This area near Vandeventer Flat was a traditional area for gathering Opuntia cacti.

Pinyon Gathering Area, Black Hill (182)

The top of Black Hill was an important site for gathering pinyon nuts, a major Cahuilla staple (Bean and Saubel 1972:102).

Pinyon Gathering Area, Little Pinyon Flat (180)

This area was an important site for gathering pinyon nuts (Pinus monophylla and Pinus quadrifolia), major Cahuilla staples (Bean and Saubel 1972:102).

Pinyon Gathering Area, Sheep Mountain Peak (181)

The peak of Sheep Mountain was an important site for gathering pinyon nuts (Bean and Saubel 1972:102).

Pinyon Gathering Area, Toro Peak (177)

This site on the south slope of Toro Peak near Coyote Canyon was an important area for pinyon nut harvesting for the Cahuilla (Bean and Saubel 1972:102).

Pinyon Gathering Area, Tu' tu' (281)

This area on Coyote Creek was a traditional gathering area for pinyon nuts.

Pinyon Gathering Area, Upper Deep Canyon (178)

Abundant stands of pinyon trees were found in the "upper reaches of Deep Canyon" and were important for the Cahuilla of the area (Bean and Saubel 1972:102).

Serviceberry Gathering Area, Pipes Canyon (167)

Among the berries utilized by the Cahuilla was the serviceberry, Amelanchier pallida. One of the places where it has been found is on the Pipes Canyon road (Bean and Saubel 1972:38).

Serviceberry Gathering Area, Toro Canyon (171)

One of the places where serviceberries (Amelanchier pallida) have been observed, and where they were gathered by the Cahuilla is near Toro Canyon (Bean and Saubel 1972: 38).

Yucca Gathering Area, Eastern Santa Rosa Mountains (185)

This whole general area was used by the Cahuilla as a yucca gathering area. The Mohave Yucca, Yucca achidigera (Cahuilla name--hunuvat), grows abundantly there. Fruit pods of this yucca are from three to five inches long and about an inch in diameter. They are eaten after being roasted. The roots of the plant were scraped for soap, and its fiber was of an excellent quality for many textile purposes. The leaves were used in construction of buildings, and the seeds were used for women's necklaces (Bean and Saubel 1972:151-152).

Name of Site	CSRI No.	Arch. Site Record No.	USGS Topographic Map	Study Area
Paltūkwic kaīkaīawit	1		Oasis quad	Near primary
Īviatim	2		Oasis quad	Primary
Travertine Palms Wash	3		Oasis quad	Primary and secondary
Rattlesnake Spring	4		Font's Pt. Quad	Secondary
Cottonwood Spring	5		Clark Lake Quad	Primary
Hidden Spring	6		Clark Lake Quad	Secondary
Virgin Spring, Trail	7		Palm Desert Quad	Secondary
Cedar Spring	8	Riv-304,389	Palm Desert Quad	Secondary
Stump Spring	9		Palm Desert Quad	Secondary
Santa Rosa Spring	10		Palm Desert Quad	Secondary
Mountain Home Spring	11		Palm Desert Quad	Secondary
Cactus Spring Area	12	Riv-1328,8217,822	Palm Desert Quad	Secondary
Cactus Spring Trail	13		Palm Desert Quad	Secondary
Agua Alta Spring	14		Palm Desert Quad	Secondary
Coyote Creek	15	(Riv-422-425; 427,429, 430-432,441,445,451, 454,457,458,498,499)	Palm Desert Quad	Near secondary
Old Santa Rosa Ruins	16	Riv-200	Clark Lake Quad	Secondary
Bear Creek Palms	17		Palm Desert Quad	Primary
Cahuilla Village	18		Palm Springs Quad	Primary
Palhīliwit	19		Coachella Quad	Within 1 mile of primary
Temelsēkalet	20		Coachella Quad	Within 1 mile of primary

Name of Site	CSRI No.	Arch. Site Record No.	USGS Topographic Map	Study Area
Temelmekmekuka	21		Coachella Quad	Within 1 mile of primary
Puichekiva	22		Coachella Quad	Within 2 miles of Study Area
Mauulmii	23		Coachella Quad	Near Primary
Eit	24	Riv-308,309	Idyllwild and Palm Springs Quads	Primary
Sewitckul	25		Palm Springs and Idyllwild Quads	Primary
Panyik	26		Palm Springs Quad	Primary
Cottonwood Springs Village Ruins	27		Clark Lake Quad	Primary
Asbestos Spring	28		Palm Desert Quad	Secondary
Dos Palmas Spring	29		Palm Desert Quad	Primary
Potrero Spring	30	Riv-580,1618,1620	Palm Desert Quad	Primary
Magnesia Spring	31		Palm Desert Quad	Primary
Agua Bonita Spring	32		Idyllwild Quad	Near Primary
Chaparrosa Spring	33		Morongo Valley Quad	Within 1 mile of secondary
Fish Traps	34	Riv-7,10	Coachella Valley	Primary
Fish Trap Petroglyphs	35		Coachella Quad	Primary
Toro Cemetery	36		Coachella Valley	Primary
Hidden Gulch Palms	37		Palm Springs Quad	Near primary

Name of Site	CSRI No.	Arch. Site Record No.	USGS Topographic Map	Study Area
Big Falls	38		Idyllwild Quad	Near primary
Toro Wells	39		Coachella Quad	Primary
Clark Lake Rock Feature	40		Clark Lake Quad	Within 1 mile of secondary
Archaeological Site of Clark Lake Dune Village	41		Clark Lake Quad	Within 1 mile of secondary
Clark Lake Petroglyphs	42		Clark Lake Quad	Secondary
Clark Lake Petroglyph Trail	43T		Clark Lake Quad	Secondary and primary
Olla Cache	44		Clark Lake Quad	Primary
Ataki, Hidden Spring Village	45		Clark Lake Quad	Secondary
Petroglyphs in Rock-house Canyon	46	Near Riv-15	Clark Lake Quad	Primary
Andreas Canyon Trail	47		Palm Springs Quad	Primary
West Fork, Palm Canyon Hunting Trail	48		Idyllwild Quad	Primary
Tev ing el we wy wen it	49		Idyllwild Quad	Primary
Pinyon Flat	50	Riv-203,388	Palm Desert Quad	Secondary, in part
Painted Sign Marks in Andreas Canyon	51		Idyllwild Quad	Primary
Kaunukvela	52			
Tūva	54		Oasis Quad	Near primary and secondary

Name of Site	CSRI No.	Arch. Site Record No.	USGS Topographic Map	Study Area
Palo Verde Spring	56		Font's Point Quad	Secondary
Rock Tanks	57		Font's Point Quad	Secondary
Little Clark Lake	58		Font's Point Quad	Within 1 mile of secondary
Village Site	59		Clark Lake Quad	Outside Study Area
(New) Santa Rosa, Sewia, or Sewiu, or We-wut-now-hu	60		Palm Desert Quad	Secondary
Mission Creek home of Kilyiñakiktum clan	61		Palm Springs Quad	
Haviñavitcum territory	63		Palm Springs Quad	Outside study area
Toro	64	Associated with Riv-9, 273, 369, 764, 1331, 1332, 1340-1344, 1346-1351	Coachella Valley	Primary
Kahvinish, Indian Wells	69		Palm Desert Quad	Not in Study Area
Kwa le ki	70		Palm Desert Quad	Near secondary
Isilsiveyaiutcem	78		Coachella Quad	Primary
Weal um mo Mountain, Santa Rosa Mountain	84		Palm Desert Quad	Secondary
Cow on vah al ham ah	85		Palm Desert Quad	Not in Study Area
Ta co wits, Taquitz Mountain	86		Palm Springs Quad	Not in Study Area
San we yet, Vandeventer Flat	89		Idyllwild Quad	Near secondary
Magnesia Spring Canyon	90		Palm Desert Quad	Primary

Name of Site	CSRI No.	Arch. Site Record No.	USGS Topographic Map	Study Area
Ca wish is mal, Cathedral Canyon	91		Thousand Palms Quad	Primary
Palms to Pines Trail	92		Palm Desert Quad	Primary
Milyillikalet	93		Palm Springs Quad	Primary
Telkic	94		Palm Springs Quad	Primary
Wa wish ca le it	95		Thousand Palms Quad	Primary
Na hal log wen et, Snow Creek	96		Palm Springs Quad	Not in Study Area
San Gorgonio Pass	110		Palm Springs Quad	Near secondary
Kawishmu	111		Palm Springs Quad	Near secondary
Andreas Canyon Village	125	Riv-516,517,518	Palm Springs Quad	Primary
Deep Canyon	128	Riv-204-207,371,428, 433-440,442,443,444, 446-450,453,456,459-462, 465-469,500,501,562,563, 566,795,1327,1367	Palm Desert Quad	Primary
Hermit's Bench Palm Oasis	156	Riv-165	Idyllwild Quad	Primary
Palm Canyon Trail Shrines	157	Riv-97, 97T	Idyllwild Quad	Primary
"Fig Tree John" Petroglyphs	158		Oasis Quad	Primary
Travertine Rocks Cave and Petroglyphs	159		Oasis Quad	Near primary and secondary
Juan Razon's Allotment	163		Oasis Quad	Near primary
Village Cremation Site	164		Clark Lake Quad	Primary

Name of Site	CSRI No.	Arch. Site Record No.	USGS Topographic Map	Study Area
Trail in Rockhouse Valley	165 T		Clark Lake Quad	Primary
Pipes Canyon Serviceberry Gathering area	167		Morongo Valley Quad	Secondary
Whitewater Canyon Agave-gathering area	168		Morongo Valley Quad	Secondary
Deep Canyon Agave-gathering area	169		Palm Desert Quad	Primary
Rabbit Peak Agave-gathering Area	170		Rabbit Peak Quad	Primary
Toro Canyon Service-berry Gathering Area	171		Palm Desert Quad	Primary
Manzanita Gathering Area	172		Clark Lake Quad	Primary
Rockhouse Valley Peppergrass Gathering Area	173		Clark Lake Quad	Primary
Barrel Cactus Gathering Area, Santa Rosa Mts.	174		Clark Lake Quad	Secondary
Whitewater Canyon Barrel Cactus Gathering Area	175		Palm Springs Quad	Secondary
Bottle Gourd, Rockshelter	176		Palm Desert Quad	Primary
Toro Peak Pinyon Nut Gathering Area	177		Palm Desert Quad	Secondary

Name of Site	CSRI No.	Arch. Site Record No.	USGS Topographic Map	Study Area
Upper Deep Canyon Pinyon Nut Gathering Area	178		Palm Desert Quad	Secondary
Little Pinyon Flat Pinyon Gathering Area	180		Palm Desert Quad	Primary and secondary
Sheep Mountain Peak Pinyon Gathering Area	181		Palm Desert Quad	Primary
Black Hill Pinyon Gathering Area	182		Palm Desert Quad	Primary
Mesquite Gathering Area, Rockhouse Canyon	183		Clark Lake Quad	Secondary
Acorn Gathering Area, Upper Murray Canyon	184		Idyllwild Quad	Primary
Yucca Gathering Area, Eastern Santa Rosa Mts.	185		Coachella Quad	Primary
Possible Site of Early Agricultural Beginnings	186		Rabbit Peak Quad	Primary
Palukiki, Stubbe Canyon	188	Associated with Riv-261T	Palm Springs Quad	Secondary
Wanüp	189	Probably associated with Riv-75,81,261T	Palm Springs Quad	Secondary
Yamisevul, Mission Creek Area	190		Morongo Valley Quad	Secondary
Mukunpat	191		Morongo Valley Quad	Secondary
Pa-nach-sa	193		Palm Desert	Primary

Name of Site	CSRI No.	Arch. Site Record No.	USGS Topographic Map	Study Area
Maringa	197		Morongo Val. Quad	Secondary
Tüirka	198		Morongo Val. Quad	
Village Site	200		Coachella Quad	Near primary
Nicholias Canyon, Spring, & Village	203		Clark Lake Quad	Secondary
Fat mel mo	205		Palm Springs Quad	Primary
Lake Cahuilla Shoreline	206		Oasis Quad	Primary
Palm Canyon Trail	207T		Idyllwild and Palm Springs Quads	Primary
"Gordon Trail"	209		Palm Springs Quad	Primary
Dead Indian Creek Oasis	210		Palm Desert Quad	Primary
Upper Dead Indian Creek Trail	211		Palm Desert Quad	Primary
Grapevine Creek Palm Oasis	212		Palm Desert Quad	Primary
"One Palm Creek"	213		Palm Desert Quad	Primary
Hidden Palms Creek Palm Oasis	214		Palm Desert Quad	Primary
Bear Creek Palm Oasis	215		Palm Desert Quad	Primary
Pictograph Site	216	Riv-68	Palm Springs Quad	Primary
Pa:tsh yara:'nka' Wanet	217		Morongo Val. Quad	Secondary

Name of Site	CSRI No.	Arch. Site Record No.	USGS Topographic Map	Study Area
La Quinta	218		Palm Desert Quad	Within 1 mile of primary
Devil's Garden	219		Palm Springs Quad	Secondary
Tevin' imulwi-waiwinut	220	Possibly associated with Riv-1097	Palm Springs Quad	Primary
Paskwa	221		Idyllwild Quad	Primary
Tatmilmi	222		Idyllwild Quad	Near Study Area
Sewi	223		Idyllwild Quad	Near Study Area
Simuta	224		Idyllwild Quad	Primary
Pinalata, Kalahal	225		Idyllwild Quad	Primary
Tcial	226		Idyllwild Quad	Primary
Kaukwicheki	227		Idyllwild Quad	Primary
Pulukla	228		Idyllwild Quad	Within 1 mile of primary
Taupakic	230		Palm Desert Quad	Primary
Indio Mountain	232		Palm Desert Quad	Primary
Kauissimtcem hempki	233		Palm Springs Quad	Primary
Temukvall	234		Palm Springs Quad	Within 1 mile of primary
Wilamu	273		Palm Desert Quad	Secondary
Con kish wi qual	274		Palm Springs Quad	Within 1 mile of secondary

Name of Site	CSRI No.	Arch. Site Record No.	USGS Topographic Map	Study Area
Hiawat	275		Palm Desert, Clark Lake, and Rabbit Peak Quads	Primary
Trail from Clark Dry Lake to Rabbit Peak	278T	Riv-166	Clark Lake and Rabbit Peak Quads	Secondary
Vandeventer Flat Gathering Area for Greens	279		Idyllwild Quad	Within 1 mile of Secondary
Tu' tu', Pinyon Gathering Area	281		Idyllwild Quad	Near secondary
Opuntia Gathering Area	282		Idyllwild Quad	Near secondary
Well No. 1	285		Idyllwild Quad	Near secondary
Murray Hills Trail	287		Thousand Palms Quad	Near primary
Martinez Canyon	288	Riv-4,313-316, 823-835,1333, 1335,1336,1345,1594	Coachella Quad	Primary
Palpūniviktum hemkĭ	291		Coachella Quad	Near primary
Tcĭuk	293			Location unknown
You koo hul ya me	294		Idyllwild Quad	Primary
Sim mo ta, or Tev koo hul ya me	295	Riv-598,599	Idyllwild Quad	Primary
Gash mo	297		Palm Springs Quad	Primary
Ūakĭ	298			Location unknown
Springs	301		Palm Desert Quad	Secondary
Martinez Mountain	303	Riv-1621-1624	Palm Desert Quad	Secondary

Name of Site	CSRI No.	Arch. Site Record No.	USGS Topographic Map	Study Area
Bradley Canyon	305		Palm Desert Quad	Primary
Horse Portrero Canyon	306		Palm Desert Quad	Primary
Haystack Mountain	307		Palm Desert Quad	Primary
Ebbens Creek	308	Riv-1608,1609	Palm Desert Quad	Primary
Carrizo Creek	310		Palm Desert Quad	Primary
Bear Creek and Trail	312	Riv-8917	Palm Desert Quad	Primary
Devil Canyon	313	Riv-37	Palm Desert Quad	Primary
Guadalupe Creek	314		Palm Desert Quad	Primary
Agua Alta Canyon	315	Riv-1588-1593, 1595	Coachella and Palm Desert Quads	Primary
Casa de Cuerva	317		Coachella and Palm Desert Quads	Primary
Bullseye Rock	318		Idyllwild Quad	Primary
Mad Woman Spring	319		Idyllwild Quad	Primary
Indian Spring	322		Idyllwild Quad	Primary
Agua Fuerte Spring	323		Idyllwild Quad	Primary
Alder Canyon	325		Clark Lake Quad	Secondary
Buck Ridge	326		Clark Lake Quad	Secondary
Jackass Flat	327		Clark Lake Quad	Secondary
Sheep Canyon	328		Rabbit Peak Quad	Primary

Name of Site	CSRI No.	Arch. Site Record No.	USGS Topographic Map	Study Area
Rattlesnake Canyon	329		Font's Point Quad	Secondary
Palo Verde Canyon	331		Font's Point Quad	Secondary
Smoke Tree Canyon	332		Font's Point Quad	Secondary
Cottonwood Canyon	334	Riv-73, Serrano village site	Palm Springs Quad	Secondary
Cox Ranch	337		Palm Springs Quad	Secondary
Forks Spring	338		Morongo Val. Quad	Secondary
Mission Creek Trail	340		Morongo Val. Quad	Secondary
Still's Landing and Millard Canyon Trail	344		Morongo Val. Quad	Secondary
Sherman Shady Spring	345		Morongo Val. Quad	Near secondary
Pierce Ranch and Springs	346		Morongo Val. Quad	Secondary
Trail from Horse Canyon to Hidden Spring	347T		Clark Lake Quad	Secondary
Trail from Middle Willows to Hidden Spring	348T		Clark Lake Quad	Secondary
Trail from Coyote Canyon to Hidden Spring	349T		Clark Lake Quad	Secondary
Trail to Clark Lake and Hidden Spring	350T		Clark Lake Quad	Secondary
Trail and associated Features	351T		Font's Point and Seventeen Palms Quads	Secondary
Rock Tanks	352		Font's Point Quad	Secondary

Name of Site	CSRI No.	Arch. Site Record No.	USGS Topographic Map	Study Area
Watering Place for Wildlife	353		Clark Lake Quad	Secondary
Trail between Nicolas Canyon and Santa Rosa Reservation	354T		Clark Lake and Palm Desert Quads	Secondary
Trail from Rockhouse Valley to Toro Peak	355T		Palm Desert Quad	Secondary

REFERENCES

Anonymous

    ca. 1938   Cahuilla Sites in Northeastern San Diego County.
                  Site records in files of L. J. Bean.

Baldwin, Clifford Park

    1938   Toro Reservation Indian Wells. The Masterkey
                  12:151-153, 157.

Bancroft, Hubert Howe

    1883-   The Native Races of the Pacific States. 5 vols.
    1886   San Francisco: A. L. Bancroft & Company.

    1886-   History of California, 1854-1890. 7 vols.
    1890   San Francisco: A. L. Bancroft & Company.

Barrows, David P.

    1893-   The Coahuilla Indians. Manuscript, in file of
    1900   L. J. Bean.

    1900   The Ethno-Botany of the Coahuilla Indians of
                  Southern California. Chicago: University of
                  Chicago Press.

Bean, Lowell John

    1959   Field notes, in files of author.

    ca. 1960   Cahuilla field notes, in files of author.

    1960   The Wanakik Cahuilla. The Masterkey 34:111-120.

    1966   California Fan Palm Sites. Manuscript, in files
                  of author.

    1972   Mukat's People: The Cahuilla Indians of Southern
                  California. Berkeley: University of California
                  Press.

    1976   Power and Its Applications in Native California.
                  In Native Californians: A Theoretical Retrospec-
                  tive. Lowell J. Bean and Thomas C. Blackburn, eds.
                  Pp. 407-420. Ramona, California: Ballena Press.

Bean, Lowell John

    1978   Cahuilla. In Handbook of North American Indians.
                  Vol. 8 (California). William C. Sturtevant, gen.
                  ed., Robert F. Heizer, vol. ed. Pp. 575-587.
                  Washington: Smithsonian Institution.

Bean, Lowell John, and William Marvin Mason

    1962   The Romero Expedition, 1823-1826. Los Angeles:
                  Ward Ritchie Press.

Bean, Lowell John, and Katherine Siva Saubel

    1972   Temalpakh: Cahuilla Knowledge and Usage of
                  Plants. Banning, California: Malki Museum Press.

Bean, Lowell John, and Sylvia Brakke Vane, eds.

    1978   Persistence and Power: A Study of Native American
                  Peoples in the Sonoran Desert and the Devers-Palo
                  Verde High Voltage Transmission Line. Report
                  prepared for Southern California Edison Company
                  by Cultural Systems Research, Inc. Rosemead,
                  California: Southern California Edison Company.

    1979a   Native Americans of Western Riverside County,
                  California and the Devers-Mira Loma 500 kV Trans-
                  mission Line Route (Lamb Canyon-Mira Loma Section).
                  Report prepared for Southern California Edison
                  Company by Cultural Systems Research, Inc.
                  Rosemead, California: Southern California Edison
                  Company.

    1979b   Cultural Resources and the High Voltage Transmission
                  Line from San Onofre to Santiago Substation and
                  Black Star Canyon: A Study of the Ethnography,
                  Archaeology, and History of the Vicinity of the
                  Line. Report prepared for Southern California
                  Edison Company by Cultural Systems Research, Inc.
                  Rosemead, California: Southern California Edison
                  Company.

Beidler, Peter G.

    1977   Fig Tree John: An Indian in Fact and Fiction.
                  Tucson: University of Arizona Press.

Benedict, Ruth

    1924   A Brief Sketch of Serrano Culture. American
                  Anthropologist 26:366-392.

Bennett, Melba

    1948   Field notes, in files of L. J. Bean.

Chase, J. Smeaton

    1919   California Desert Trails. Boston: Houghton
                Mifflin.

Curtis, Edward S.

    1926   The North American Indian, Vol. 15. Norwood,
                Massachusetts: Plimpton Press. (Johnson Reprint,
                New York, 1970.)

Drucker, Philip

    1937   Culture Element Distributions V: Southern
                California. University of California Anthropo-
                logical Records 1:1-52.

Gifford, Edward Winslow

    1918   Clans and Moieties in Southern California.
                University of California Publications in American
                Archaeology and Ethnology 14:155-219.

Henderson, Randall

    1941   Waterfall in Palm Canyon. Desert Magazine
                (January).

    1961   Let's Hike to Where the Palms Grow Wild: 10 Oases
                in the Canyons Above Palm Desert. Desert Magazine,
                April, 24-26.

Hooper, Lucile

    1920   The Cahuilla Indians. University of California
                Publications in American Archaeology and Ethno-
                logy 16:315-380. (Reprinted in Studies in Cahuilla
                Culture, Malki Museum Press, Banning, California,
                1978.)

Jaeger, Edmund C.

    1953   Forgotten Trails. Palm Springs Villager, Septem-
                ber, pp. 12-14, 28.

James, George Wharton

    1908   Through Ramona's Country. Boston: Little, Brown.

    1918   The Wonders of the Colorado Desert. Boston: Little, Brown.

James, Harry C.

    1960   The Cahuilla Indians. Banning, California: Malki Museum Press.

Johnston, Francis J.

    1960   Archaeological Problems of the Eastern Wanakik Territory. Manuscript in files of L. J. Bean.

    1977   The Bradshaw Trail: Narrative and Notes. Riverside: Historical Commission Press.

Klein, Jack

    Date   The Lady of the Palo Verde Tree. Los Angeles:
    unknown   Los Angeles Sunday Times.

Kroeber, A. L.

    1907   Shoshonean Dialects of California. University of California Publications in American Archaeology and Ethnology 4:65-165.

    1908   Ethnography of the Cahuilla Indians. University of California Publications in American Archaeology and Ethnology 8:1-68. (Reprinted in Studies in Cahuilla Culture, Malki Museum Press, Banning, California, 1978.)

    1909   Notes on Shoshonean Dialects of Southern California. University of California Publications in American Archaeology and Ethnology 8:253-256.

    1916   California Place Names of Indian Origin. Berkeley: University of California Publications in American Archaeology and Ethnology 12(2):31-69.

    1925   Handbook of the Indians of California. Bureau of American Ethnology, Bulletin 78. (Dover Publications, New York, 1976.)

Lawton, Harry

    1960   Willie Boy: A Desert Manhunt. Balboa Island,
               California: The Paisano Press.

Lawton, Harry, and Lowell John Bean

    1968   A Preliminary Reconstruction of Aboriginal
               Agricultural Technology Among the Cahuilla.
               The Indian Historian 1(5):18-24, 29.

Meighan, Clement W.

    1959   Varieties of Prehistoric Cultures in the Great
               Basin Region. Southwest Museum, Masterkey 33:
               46-59.

Merriam, Clinton Hart

    Date   Ethnographic Field Notes, on file at Bancroft
    unknown   Library, University of California, Berkeley.

Patencio, Francisco

    1943   Stories and Legends of the Palm Springs Indians.
               Margaret Boynton, ed. Los Angeles: Times
               Mirror Company.

    1971   Desert Hours with Chief Patencio, as Told to
               Kate Collins by Chief Francisco Patencio. Roy F.
               Hudson, ed. Palm Springs: Palm Springs Desert
               Museum.

Phillips, George Harwood

    1975   Chiefs and Challengers: Indian Resistance and
               Cooperation in Southern California. Berkeley:
               University of California Press.

Reed, Lester

    1963   Old Time Cattlemen and Other Pioneers of the
               Anza-Borrego Area. Benson, Arizona: Border-
               Mountain Press. (2nd edition, 1977)

Romero, John Bruno

    1954   The Botanical Lore of the California Indians.
               With Sidelights on Historical Incidents in Cali-
               fornia. New York: Vantage Press.

Saunders, Charles Francis

1913   Under the Sky in California. New York: McBride,
            Nast & Company.

1914   With Flowers and Trees in California. New York:
            McBride, Nast & Company.

Seiler, Hansjakob

1970   Cahuilla Texts with an Introduction. Blooming-
            ton: Indiana University Language Science
            Monographs 6.

Shipek, Florence C.

1977   A Strategy for Change: The Luiseño of Southern
            California. Ph.D. dissertation, University of
            Hawaii, Honolulu.

Smith, Desmond Mohler

1942   The Effect of the Dessication of Ancient Cahuilla
            Lake Upon the Culture and Distribution of Some of
            the Desert Indians of Southern California. M.A.
            thesis, University of Southern California, Los
            Angeles.

Smith, Gerald A., and Wilson G. Turner

1975   Indian Rock Art of Southern California with
            Selected Petroglyph Catalog. Redlands: San
            Bernardino County Museum Association.

Smith, Wayland H.

1909   In Re California Indians to Date. Los Angeles
            Council of the Sequoyah League Bulletin No. 5.

Steward, J. H.

1929   Petroglyphs of California and Adjoining States.
            University of California Publications in American
            Archaeology and Ethnology 24:47-238.

Strong, William Duncan

1929   Aboriginal Society in Southern California.
            University of California Publications in American
            Archaeology and Ethnology 26. (Malki Museum Press,
            Banning, California, 1972.)

U.S. Department of Commerce, Bureau of the Census

    1860

U.S. Department of the Interior, Bureau of Land Management

    1978   Ethnographic Notes 22.

Vane, Sylvia Brakke

    1970   Field notes, in files of author.

    1979   Field notes, in CSRI files.

Walsh, Jane MacLaren

    1976   John Peabody Harrington: The Man and his California Indian Fieldnotes. Ramona, California: Ballena Press.

Wilke, Philip J.

    1976   Late Prehistoric Human Ecology at Lake Cahuilla, Coachella Valley, California. Ph.D. dissertation, University of California, Riverside.

Wilke, Philip J., and Harry W. Lawton

    1975   Early Observations on Cultural Geography of Coachella Valley. Ramona, California: Ballena Press Anthropological Papers No. 3.